THE INNOCENTS AT HOME

Children of the 1940s

MARY STONE

While the accounts in this collection are based upon actual events or circumstances of the 1940s, the narratives, names and characters in the stories are fictional and do not resemble any real person living or deceased.

The Innocents at Home—Children of the 1940s
Copyright © 2024 by Mary Stone

Paperback ISBN 979-8-9888863-6-5
Ebook ISBN 979-8-9888863-7-2

Front Cover and Interior Design/Formatting By: Richell Balansag

Also by Mary Stone

Non-Fiction

*Run in the Path of Peace—the Secret of
Being Content No Matter What*

*When Your Wife Gets on Your Nerves—
or Worse; 52 Verses to Bolster You*

*When Your Husband is a Christian—But Doesn't
Always Act Like One; 52 Verses to Lift You Up*

*When You Have an Unsaved Loved One—
52 Devotions to Give You Hope*

Fiction

In BeTWEEN TROUBLE

ACCLAIM FOR

THE INNOCENTS AT HOME

Children of the 1940s

The depth of Mary Stone's research for *The Innocents at Home—Children of the 1940s*, and her ability to capture the perspectives of children with respect and realism is impressive! In this book, familial relationships are complex and heartfelt. The author has a good ear for dialogue.—Jon Gosch, award-winning author of *Deep Fire Rise* and *If We Get There*.

The Innocents at Home—Children of the 1940s evokes many memories for readers. Creative, fun games children in the 1940s conceived to entertain themselves is just one example. Conversely, the book includes situations of this decade that were scary for children, e.g. war, disease, and internment camps, to name a few. The stories relate real-life incidents that were an integral part of this era. Author Mary Stone's descriptions and dialogue are so well written one actually sees the narratives play out. Readers will become involved in each of the eighteen stories because the characters are extraordinarily real.—Judy Heitkotter, Book Reviewer for *The Reflection Ridge Living Magazine*, Wichita, Kansas.

If you ever wondered what impact war has on the lives of the young, *The Innocents at Home* by Mary Stone is a great place to discover the answer. This collection of vignettes presents thought-provoking experiences of children growing up in the 1940s who lived the ravages of war. From Toulouse, France to Dekator, Alabama, to an internment camp in Crystal City, Texas, the reader is drawn in to share in bewilderment, personal loss, bullying, kindness, poverty, discrimination and triumph. I was particularly impressed by the level of research the author had to have done to compile such a group of intense stories. Rarely is an author able to deliver such simple incidents while captivating the reader with an emotional understanding of the lives and minds of children. This book is fresh, intense and powerful and I highly recommend it!—Joye Haneberg, Retired Banker

ACKNOWLEDGEMENTS

"Brooklyn vs. the Bronx" earned Honorable Mention in *Rambunctious Review*'s 2002 fiction contest.

"Brooklyn vs. the Bronx" Placed First in Ocean Shores "Write on the Beach" contest in 2004.

"Upstart or New Start" was awarded Honorable Mention in *Rambunctious Review*'s 2005 fiction contest.

"Going Places," was first published in *The Salal Review*, Volume 9: Spring 2009.

In 2012, OakTara Publishing included a revised version of "Going Places" under a new title, "Foreign Feelings," in its anthology, *I Choose You*.

"Internment Camp" placed Honorable Mention in *Rambunctious Review*'s 2012 fiction contest.

A BOUQUET OF APPRECIATION

I extend my utmost gratitude to those who joined me in this journey, through critiquing, encouraging, and providing invaluable insight and feedback.

To all of you, Charolette Conklin, Margaret Miller, Lori Steed, Adam Wolfer, Patrick Kubin, Dan Roberts, Ed Putka, Judy Heitkotter, and Meg Stone, I say, "Thank you for your inspiration and support to keep writing."

Most of all, thank you, Lord Jesus, for your help every step of the way in this writing. Without You, this project would not have been possible.

PREFACE

This collection is a culmination of lengthy research and many years in the making. I interviewed those whose childhoods subsisted in the 1940s. I attended numerous speaking engagements presented by people who experienced the circumstances of this decade. I spent countless hours in our local library poring over archives, volumes of historical statistics, microfiche reels, books, and magazines, two of which included *Life* and *Saturday Evening Post*.

These resources provided instrumental inspiration, along with factual details—although in some cases, I crafted scenarios that diverged from actuality to fit the story—for each of the eighteen narratives in this compilation. While the stories are based on real events and circumstances which transpired during the 1940s, the characters and storylines are figments of my imagination, and in no way resemble real persons, living or deceased.

Having relied on my many years as a Counselor listening and understanding people—hearing their inner child—as I crafted each story, I delved into the mind's eye and heart of each child as (s)he recounted his or her experiences of turmoil, trials, losses, and triumphs encountered and endured during this time in history.

I hope you, dear readers, recognize and *feel* the impact of this era on children from various parts of the globe—regions of the United States of America, Poland, Germany, and France—in this multicultural anthology. The children within these pages are of various descents—American, German, Polish, French, Japanese, and German. I pray the stories show how prejudice and preconceived beliefs about people from different ethnicities and cultures are just as destructive as is a world war.

As I began crafting these stories, my mind exploded into "What ifs?" and "What would it be like to . . . ?"

- What if a daughter were sent to live with her Nazi Commandant father in his extermination camp?
- What would it be like to hide from the enemy in a damp, dark cave in Poland for a year, without seeing the light of day for this whole time?
- What would a German teen go through while living in Iowa during this time?
- What would it be like for a Japanese teenager to be ripped from her home on the west coast to be sent to live in an Internment Camp in Texas?
- What would happen when German POWs were sent to your parents' farm to help with the crops?

As I explored these and many more issues, my characters spoke to me in the telling of their stories. Thank you for investing your time and interest in hearing them speak to you.

Mary Stone

CONTENTS

"FOOTSTEPS IN THE NIGHT"

1940
Paris, then Toulouse, France

I heard the uncertainty in *mon père's* voice as he spoke with *Maman.* "Hitler's soldiers now occupy the north of France. We can no longer afford our life of luxury in an Occupied Zone."

Maman saw my eyes peering around the door to the dining room. She looked at *Papa* and pressed a finger to her lips. Ushering me upstairs to my bedroom, she admonished me in a firm yet gentle voice, "Nine-year-old ears do not need to hear such things." With that, she closed the door.

Her footfalls descended the steps. Quietly, I inched the door open and sneaked to the stairwell landing, making certain to stay out of sight.

"...surely as a successful industrialist, your employer need not transfer you to the south of France—into the Free Zone." I heard the tremor in *ma mère's* voice.

I wondered about the difference between a Free Zone and an Occupied one.

Within days, *Papa* set out to relocate us, approaching this change with a sense of adventure. "Nicolette," he said, "we will have many new streets, museums, and shops to explore.

Perhaps in a store window sits a doll with golden curls waiting for you—one with big blue eyes and golden tresses."

Some of my friends thought me too old for dolls. *Maman* scoffed at such nonsense. I agreed. Besides, I longed for a doll that looked like me. Even though my older sister no longer played with hers, she had a doll with long black hair like hers. I had *ma mère's* Scandinavian hair coloring and *mon père's* curls. *Maman* kept my hair short; she said it was much easier to tame that way.

Excitement and anticipation motioned me into the limousine transporting *Papa*, *Maman*, Michelle—a year older and Miche to me, (pronounced Meesh)—two-year-old Françoise, my cat *Ronron*, and me off to Toulouse, France.

"*Au revoir, Paris*," *Maman* whispered.

We crawled through tangled traffic along *Le Champs-Elysée* and toward the route heading south. A tear spilled down *ma mère's* cheek. *Papa* pulled a handkerchief from his suit pocket, unfolded it, and gently wiped the drop from her face.

"*Ma Chérie*," he said, "the Germans will not be here long. In all the history of France, no country has proven strong enough to conquer the French. This is but a minor invasion, a mere blemish on the face of freedom." He tenderly kissed her hand. "We will return . . . and be much the better for it." His words were like a warm *duvet* to me. The tone of his voice and confidence in his eyes told me he held the truth.

Maman sighed and squeezed his hand. Closing her eyelids, she hummed, then sang to us girls our favorite song, "*Les Cloches de Harlème*." It beat with a tinge of sadness, yet rang for us a hint of hope on our journey away from familiarity. *Maman's* sadness spilled over into my lap while *Papa's* hope lifted me enough to peer out the window and glimpse vistas beyond my *environs* that I had never known.

Tiny towns peppered the countryside. Gone was the pace of Paris. Farmers plodded along in horse-drawn carts. Women wore scarves rather than fashionable hats, and lacked a rush to their steps. Fewer motorcars, but many *bicyclettes* roamed the roads. Green pastures spread like tablecloths over hillsides offering a picnic of grass to herds of cattle and sheep. It felt peaceful, although unusual. The drive lulled me to sleep.

* * * * *

"Nicolette." *Maman* shook me gently. As I opened my eyes, my first sight was of *Papa* carrying Françoise into our new home. Beside him skipped Miche—always the bravest and most curious—who dashed ahead to beat everyone to the door.

We spent the day exploring every nook and cranny of the dwelling. Larger than our apartment in Paris, it offered much room to run and play hide-and-seek. *Maman* busied herself putting our clothes away into closets and drawers. *Papa* left to report to his new place of work.

The following morning, *Maman* dressed us for a walk to the local market. Canvas bags in her hands for the baguettes, cheese, and hopefully vegetables she would fill them with, she gave one last check of her hair piled atop her head in the hall mirror before closing the door behind her.

It is difficult to describe that morning, the following one, and the weeks after that. Perhaps it is best summed up in *Maman's* words. "Refugees. We are treated like refugees."

The people of Toulouse were rude to us. They must have considered our presence an invasion. Time passed, and communication with them was poor, so we were not prepared for our first experience with an air raid.

In the middle of one especially dark night, sirens pierced the air. The shrill sound drew our fear, which spilled like blood. People ran into the streets searching for shelter. We knew of no shelter, so the five of us huddled together in a room.

From that moment on, I had a sixth sense for incoming planes, even before the sirens sounded. The air raids always came at night. The planes were British, our ally, *Papa* told us, coming to bomb French factories and railroads. He explained, "The British help us by targeting France's facilities the Germans have taken over." So when bombs rained from the sky and fiery explosions resulted, although terrified, the French cheered.

After that first air raid, *Papa* located a shelter. We practiced getting out of the apartment quickly, following the same route each time. Also in preparation for the air raids, before we went to bed, *Maman* would have us fold our clothes in the reverse order of how we would dress ourselves in the dark. Shoes on the bottom, and so on, leaving our underwear on top of the pile.

One night, I startled awake. I ran to my parents' bedroom. "*Papa*, the planes are coming!"

He sprang from his bed, *Maman* right behind. Lights were forbidden. We stumbled, groping for our prepared piles. After scrambling into our clothes in the darkness, we left our house just as the sirens blared. People poured from their homes into the street. Chaos joined them. *Papa* and *Maman* firmly gripped our hands. Running in blackness was difficult, especially with the swarm of bodies banging into ours.

Part way to the shelter, I remembered *Ronron* locked in our residence. Why had we not included my pet in our raid rehearsals? I unlatched my hold from *Maman* and ran back, fighting the oncoming throng. I was not afraid for myself, only for my cat. When I arrived at our place, I tried the door, but it was locked. I pushed and pushed. It would not budge. I ran to the neighbors. They were not home. When I finally realized I would not be able to rescue my pet, I returned to the street and picked my way toward the shelter. How would I ever find my family in this tsunami, tossing me here and there in the dark? People pressed in upon me and smashed me between legs and arms and *derrières*. I gasped for breath. Thrust against a brick wall, I banged my head and scraped my cheek. I tasted blood. Above the roar, I heard what was surely *Papa's* voice. The panic in it seized me and squeezed the remaining bit of air from my lungs. I had never experienced fear in him before this moment.

"Nicolette!" I heard even more terror erupt from *Papa*, but I couldn't see him. Now many voices called names, none of them familiar. Many hands reached out. None of them I knew. I absorbed the terror in *Papa's* voice and was terrified because everyone was moving away from me. I was being left behind.

Shapes and shadows swirled around me and swallowed *Papa's* call. Abruptly, I was caught up in the onward wave and swept toward the shelter's entrance. Suddenly arms plucked me from the crush of the crowd. *Papa* gave a shout and scooped me up.

As he kissed my head, his voice cracked in relief. "Nicolette, I found you. *Grâce à Dieu*, I found you. The bomb explosion above glinted off your blonde hair bobbing amongst a sea of dark heads."

Flares torpedoed overhead to light the sky to expose our ally's planes. From their ground position, Germans brought down first one, then two British airplanes. Debris rained onto the streets of Toulouse. The noise terrified me. I started to cry and trembled in *Papa's* arms. He stroked my hair, tilted my head so that I might look into his eyes. "Fireworks!" he said.

"Nicolette, look at the colorful fireworks." His smile, his tone of voice, soothed and lifted my gaze to see as he did. Another flare shot into the dark. Its red tail climbed higher, higher, until it exploded, illuminating the heavens. The power of it, the magnificence of its eruption was indeed beautiful.

A woman beside us shooed children into a circle and struck up a whispered song, "*Sur le Pont d'Avignon.*" Soon, little voices joined in softly with proddings from their *mamans*. Before long, hushed music cushioned the clamor of artillery.

After a while, the sirens signaled that we could return to our homes. The safety alert—long, flat shrills—was different than the warning signal with its up-and-down wavy, ear-splitting pitches.

Upon returning home, we saw that bombs had blown the shutters off our apartment windows. Instead of lamenting, we joined our neighbors in taking chairs into the streets to sit and watch factories burn in the distance. Perhaps this was the point at which we ceased to be outsiders. My family now shared in the fear and triumphs of the Toulouse natives. The Germans and British had brought us together. No longer strangers, we were brothers and sisters.

Shortly afterwards, *Papa's* routine changed. From this point on, he often departed from our home in the evening. I frequently overheard him and *Maman* speaking in muted voices. "Germans control North of France but still . . . courting Southern France . . . French Resistance . . . underground . . . short-wave radio's messages from London . . . ."

Other changes came as well. *Papa* spoke of shipments no longer reaching Toulouse because of bombed-out railways. We had no sugar or fresh vegetables, and could only purchase milk with coupons. Even those were scarce.

Maman worried that even the French army didn't have access to precious gasoline. "It is a good thing French people are resourceful with their *bicyclettes*," she said. I wondered at the strange coal-burning machines called *gazogenes* which had suddenly appeared on the side of cars. *Papa* explained that they enabled engines to run.

Papa decided to move us to the countryside. He assured *Maman* there we could buy food on the Black Market from farmers. He was able to rent a section of a mansion—even though we were to be the only occupants—from owners who had fled to North Africa. The *château* was enormous. Rooms, rooms everywhere—many more than my sisters and I could have explored in a month. Not that we had the opportunity. We were confined to a few rooms in one wing, for that is all *Papa* had leased.

That did not stop us girls from pretending we were queens and princesses. Actually, only one of us could be Queen at a time. That honor fell to our Miche. Rather, it didn't simply fall to her. She demanded the title of "Your Royal Highness." In all honesty, she was a good Queen. Never once did she command, "Off with your heads!" Not that it would have done her any good. We siblings were only loyal to a point. Nor did she utter, "Let them eat cake." Most likely because, even though now that *Maman* was able to acquire—illegally—fruits and vegetables, not one granule of sugar could be found in the cupboards.

Had it been available for purchase, *Papa* would have laid hold of it. Instead, once a week he brought home a chocolate bar for each of us girls. Françoise always gobbled hers all at once. Miche cut hers into seven slits, one piece for each day of the week. She never went without candy. I licked mine every now and then, never biting off chunks, and was able to stretch my *bonbon* out sometimes for all of four or five days. I never intended to finish it off quite before the end of the week, but somehow it dissolved fairly quickly. I couldn't ever prove it, but I suspected I wasn't the only one savoring its milky-smooth confection.

Papa insisted that this limitation—yet an extravagance of sweets—did us no harm. *Maman* made certain we prospered in the fresh, country air. Our rosy cheeks replaced "Parisian pallor," as she called it. Our spindly legs grew into strong limbs as we climbed apple trees in the orchard just beyond the empty stable. We girls were limited only to the extent of our imaginations—and, of course, *Maman's* admonitions to not stray beyond sight of the *château*. We played damsels in distress, Napoleon and Josephine, and school—my favorite even though I was always the student. I loved to scrawl my name, Nicolette Bruiller, and read and spell lists of words. Miche attempted to teach me things I had already mastered. Although today she did teach me two new words—*vaillant* and *conspirateur*. I loved the way my top teeth pressed on my bottom lip to form the "v," and then the way my tongue took charge inside my mouth for the rest of *vaillant*. With *conspirateu*r, the little puff of "sp" that burst from my lips was fun. I repeatedly let both words roll out of my mouth. I thanked Miche for these wonderful words which meant courage and one who joins in a secret agreement.

One night our imaginations were sparked, igniting them to a whole new dimension.

Step.

Step.

Step.

The slow, deliberate footfalls proceeded down the long, wooden hallway outside our bedroom. I was the first to awaken at the ominous sound. I dared not breathe. At first I lay paralyzed, allowing only my eyes to roam. I rolled them slightly toward the door. My tongue grew thick and dried. Fear nudged me to slowly—ever so slowly and quietly—elbow Miche awake. Then, I willed one finger to emerge from under the covers to point to the door connecting our room with our parents'.

Step.

Step.

Step.

Miche threw back our *duvet,* grabbed Françoise, and bolted out of bed, leaving me to be murdered. I do not know how I got from the bed to the floor, but when I realized my feet were there, I followed my sisters, tiptoeing—lest the intruder hear us and rip off our heads. Then, half-way across the room, terrified that indeed within moments I would be headless, I froze. With the baby in one arm, Miche grabbed my arm with her other and dragged me across the cold floor. During that kilometer or so, my eyes never once left sight of the threshold to the hall. My heart hammered in my chest. I willed it to be quiet, for fear the killer would make out our progress across the room. Would he hear the ringing in my ears as well? Like a bell tolling a death knell?

When at long last she let go of my hand now but an icicle, to push me into *Papa* and *Maman's* adjoining room, my muscles thawed. I wasted no time racing to the safety of their bed. Still, my eyes fixed on the hall entrance.

Step.

Step.

The footsteps stopped just on the other side of the wall.

Squeeeeeaaak.

The doorknob turned slowly.

I couldn't swallow. My hammering heart threatened to break through my ribs. My ears thudded. I prayed the invader couldn't hear my body pounding out this clamor. I demanded my eyes to close, but they rebelled.

No-one breathed, fully expecting the appearance of an ax-wielding brute.

Papa slipped out of bed and tiptoed to the door. "Marie, is that you?" he asked, the tone of his voice lower than usual. We had, the day prior, employed a maid who moved into the servants' quarters off the kitchen.

Sloooowly, the handle turned the other way. Silence.

Step.

Step.

Step.

Footfalls echoed away down the hall and down the winding stairs.

I hardly slept the rest of the night, even though we were packed tightly against *Papa* and *Maman*. Finally morning came and light penetrated my eyelids. Only Françoise remained in bed beside me.

We scampered down the stairs to the kitchen table. A croissant awaited each of us. Apple juice, too—a treat. But I still missed cocoa powder heated with cream, sweetened with spoons of sugar. Miche waited for me to scarcely finish my breakfast before she pressed me to go exploring. I scooted back my chair. The sound of its metal legs scraping against the floor bounced back from the high ceiling and ricocheted off the bare walls.

"Mind you, do not go far," *Maman* warned.

"*Moi aussi. Moi aussi,*" begged Françoise, whom we had come to call *La Petite Ombre*—the little shadow. With *Ronron* on our heels, Miche led Françoise and me back up to the second story where she jimmied open a window. Forcing me out onto the ledge of the lower roof first, she then handed Françoise through the gap. Even though a miniature cast iron fence surrounded the edge of the roof, I clung tightly to Françoise's hand. It would not do for something bad to happen to her for two reasons, the first of which was that whenever Françoise got into trouble, somehow rather than Miche shouldering the blame, it always fell on me for the casualty. Today, I was glad Françoise's chubby little legs could not keep up with Miche's strides. After last night's near fatal attack, I was less than enthusiastic about encountering the raised and ready hatchet just around the corner.

"Shh," Miche warned, her finger to her lips. "We don't want him to know we're here," she whispered.

"Who?" I backed up, tripping over Françoise. Down we went with a thud. Françoise started to cry. I quickly clapped my hand over her mouth lest the waiting wicked beast be alerted to our presence. "Maybe we should go back," I mouthed to Miche. When she didn't get the crux of my message I pointed frantically with my free hand. She shook her head and planted her body against the *château* bricks. I glanced at Françoise. Her knee oozed red where it had scraped against the roof's walkway. I pulled her dress down over it, for if she saw the blood she would really yowl. I rose and tugged her up, my gaze now riveted on the space just ahead of Miche. She slowly crept around the corner of the mansion and disappeared. I waited for a shriek. When none came, I tucked Françoise behind me and inched forward just far enough to peer around the corner. I couldn't believe my eyes. We had discovered a tower!

"It must be Rapunzel's Tower," Miche announced.

I gulped. A thrill of adventure zinged through me and sent my heart to racing. At once, the hatchet man evaporated, and the scenario took on exciting possibilities for games to provide us with endless hours of entertainment. Drawing closer to our newfound treasure, we found the garret window was broken. Making sure we wouldn't cut ourselves, Miche removed all the splinters, cutting her finger only a little. Françoise's eyes widened and her lip quivered—until Miche sucked off the blood. That crisis solved, Miche helped us inside. Slowly, ever so slowly, we stole up the winding staircase and emerged into a little room. A single wood table and chair almost filled the small space. I sniffed the air. Cigarette odor warned us someone had been there. A small metal ashtray overflowed with butts. On top of the table a British map spread out, displaying the area of France where we now lived.

A spy! And he hadn't harmed us. We had happened upon a nice spy!

I locked eyes with Miche. She smiled. The games in which we could now engage multiplied beyond my wildest imagination. With an air of importance, Miche interrupted my budding imaginativeness. "First we must tell *Maman* of our discovery."

Returning via the path which we had come, Miche rushed off to be the one to break the exciting news, abandoning me and Françoise. When I arrived at the second story window, Françoise in tow, I saw *Maman* racing toward us, a look of terror on her face. She reached through the opening and snatched Françoise inside, hugged and kissed her, then sighed loudly. After setting the baby down, *Maman* fixed her hands on her hips. "What were you thinking taking this *enfante* out onto that treacherous walkway?"

I parted my lips to reveal the truth of the matter but was abruptly cut off.

"Go to your room, *jeune fille*. Once there, think about the danger in which you put your sister. And think about all the possibilities of harm that could have come to her because of your irresponsibility. With your imagination, no doubt, you will be able to recognize plenty."

"*Mais . . . Maman—*"

"*Allez!*"

When *Maman* used this impersonal form of the verb "go," explanations from me were fruitless. I searched the room for Miche. Of course, she was nowhere to be found. Exiled for the day, I was unable to return to the tower. That didn't stop me from venturing there in my mind. Lying in bed, I conjured up a myriad of scenarios, and none of them had anything to do with what kind of harm might have come to Françoise.

The following morning, after a night free of mysterious footfalls, *Maman* tucked us under her arms like a hen with chicks under her wings, and set out to investigate. Surveying the grounds, we proceeded to the stable. No one there. We traipsed into the orchard. No one there. At each lack of finding, *Maman* relaxed her shoulders a bit more. We expanded our search to the edge of the surrounding forest where *Maman* spied something large and white a ways off in the trees. We halted. Waited—until we were certain no one lurked in the shadows, ready to pounce on us. Obviously convinced we were not in peril, *Maman* vigilantly took one step, then another toward the object.

An exclamation escaped her lips. Her eyes watered.

I grabbed a fistful of her dress. "*Qu'est-ce que c'est?*—What is it?" I whispered, barely able to force the words past my constricted throat.

"A parachute!" The thrill in her voice excited me. "You girls each grab an armful of material."

The unwieldy bundle each of us carried as we marched back to the *château* must have been a sight. Tripping and falling, giggling and dragging one another, we had unearthed great riches—pirates bringing home buried treasure.

Maman delighted in her windfall of nylon—a rare commodity. She wasted no time cutting it into bolts and colored the cloth from dyes unearthed in the closet off the kitchen. She set about sewing beautiful blouses.

"We owe a bouquet of thanks to the British agent who landed in our woods and secreted himself in our mansion," *Maman* said upon completion of her project.

When *Papa* eventually saw what we were wearing, great concern crept into his face. However, he quickly told us how lovely we looked before taking *Maman* out of the room. I could not make out the forced whispers between them, until *Maman* raised her voice in question—"The Nazis discovered him hiding in a farmhouse nearby?"

Now I could hear *Papa's* reply. "The Germans torched the dwelling, killing not only our ally but the owners and their five children as well."

Maman's weeping spread beyond the room to me. Tears spilled down my cheeks.

Although we had never come face to face with our spy, we had come to adore him through fantasies of how he saved us from enemies. We had given him a face and a name. He was tall, dark-haired, strong, and we called him Charles Churchill, Churchill being the only British name Miche and I knew.

This catastrophe changed how we lived day to day. *Maman* developed a habit of locking and relocking doors and windows, and holding her breath at the sound of creaks in the mansion, of which there were many. *Papa*, on the other hand, seemed emboldened by the incident. No longer was he gone in the evenings to meetings. Instead, his friends appeared after dark at our back door. From there they disappeared, yet Miche and I heard men's voices long into the night—along with the faint sound of a shortwave radio.

One day after *Papa* had gone into Toulouse and *Maman* tended to Françoise who was ill, Miche grabbed my hand. "*Viens*—come, Nicolette. Today we are secret agents off in a search."

"*Pour quoi?*—For what?"

Miche emitted a gust of wind, obviously in disgust of my ignorance. She planted her hands on her hips. Already she was becoming like *Maman*. "Don't you want to find out where those voices are coming from every night?"

When challenged like that, I was ready and willing. With *Maman* taking charge of our little hanger-on-er, and the maid off to market, we were free to roam, investigate. We started at the men's point of entrance and checked every recess and alcove for secret passages. It took the better part of the morning but at last we succeeded when we sat to rest in the kitchen pantry. While Miche rummaged for something to nibble on, I plopped to the floor and leaned back against the wall under a shelf that was no taller than Françoise. When it shook, I banged my shoulder on it to make sure it was sound. That little nudge invited Miche and me into a whole other world. The panel gave way. Just inside on a ledge, sat candles and matches. Miche shoved me out of the way, lit a candle, handed it to me, then repeated the same for her. Cautiously, we crept down the narrow wood stairs, down into a cavern under the mansion. The smell of earth filled my nose and a chill wrapped around my body. I shivered, holding up my flickering light to eliminate shadows hiding monsters. And spiders.

Crates littered the grotto. A makeshift table of planks sat in the middle. On it was a candleholder with wax thick around its base, a map, and a pencil.

"Underground Resistance," Miche said in a low voice as if she knew all there was to know about anything. A great eavesdropper, my sister did have more information than I did. About some things.

This was the beginning of holding hands with espionage. The next day, Miche and I came upon a British soldier hiding under straw in the stable. Badly wounded, he could barely move. We brought him water and cheese and debated whether or not to tell *Maman*. We feared because of her nervous condition, she would not allow him to stay. So, we waited until *Papa* came home and lured him outside after dinner. From there, we led him to our spy.

"You are not to tell anyone of this," he warned. "Now, go tell your *Maman* to give you a bath."

"But I'm not dirty," I argued.

Papa grabbed a fistful of dirt and rubbed it in my hair. It smelled like horse manure. "Now you are."

Miche smiled and spread the stinky stuff onto her arms. She explained to me on the way to the mansion that this was a ruse for *Papa* to secret our spy away to another part of the *château*.

"How do you know that?" I asked, envious of her inside information.

"I guess I can trust you . . . now that you are a part of this," she said, a stern, serious look on her face. "*Papa* has been harboring injured soldiers in a part of the *château* where we are forbidden to go. Even *Maman* knows nothing of this." She halted, holding out her arm to stop me. "You must swear . . . swear . . . to not breathe a word of this to anyone. Not even to Françoise. If you do—." She glanced side to side and behind her. "*They* will come and get you and lock you up and throw away the key."

I didn't know who *they* were, and didn't want to know. Miche took me by both shoulders. "I only told you this because you are now an important part of the French Underground. We are all counting on your loyalty." I didn't like her acting like a grown up. Still, put that way, I felt important and well on my way to mimic my sister's bravery.

The next afternoon, Françoise and I were climbing trees in the orchard when a troop of Nazi soldiers marched by on the road bordering the property. Several of them waved and smiled. I waved and smiled. One of them shouted something I couldn't understand. Suddenly, they fell out of line and walked toward us. One of the ones who had waved wrapped his hands over the branch on which I was sitting. At first when he spoke, I couldn't make out what he said.

He repeated, slowly, "You . . . like . . . chocolate?" When I nodded my head, he reached into his green uniform pocket and pulled out half a bar, broke off a piece and offered it to me.

"*Merci beaucoup.*"

"*Moi aussi. Moi aussi,*" Françoise cried.

Since I had already chewed on my piece, I nodded to my sister and said to the German, "She wants one, too."

He broke off a smaller chunk and put it in her hand, then turned to survey our *château.* His brow wrinkled and looked troubled when another soldier approached.

This soldier stepped in front of the chocolate man and asked, "You . . . see . . . British," he paused then pointed upward. ". . . fall . . . from . . . sky?"

I had. In fact, there was one this very minute on the third floor of the mansion. I stared at this German soldier. His eyes were not nice like the one who had given me candy. Just as I started to answer, the chocolate man stepped between me and his comrade. He said something to the soldier with cold eyes. They laughed and left.

At bedtime, Françoise was throwing a fit because she had lost her dolly, Antoinette. I remembered it perched in the crotch of the apple tree. Running out to retrieve it, I heard a "Pssst" sound coming from the stable. By now, I had a healthy dose of courage due to Miche's tutelage and *Papa's* example, so after I rescued the doll, I dashed into the barn. The German soldier who had given me candy was crouched behind a stall. He motioned me over, placed a piece of paper in my fist. "Give . . . to . . . *Papa*," he said, then gestured me to go.

I ran for the back door, Antoinette in one hand, the message in the other. In the kitchen, I flung the doll into Françoise's lap and raced to the study where I knew *Papa* was reading. Once there, I made sure *Maman* did not follow me before I pressed the piece of paper into *Papa's* hand.

"Where did you get this?" he asked, startled.

Explaining about the German encounter, I watched his face for a clue as to the importance of the message—for I had not read it in my haste to deliver it.

Papa's forehead wrinkled. His eyes grew dark with what I had come to recognize as worry. He took me by the shoulders. "Nicolette, do not mention this to anyone. Not now, nor in the days to come." He threw on his hat and coat and dashed out the door, without kissing *Maman* goodbye. Something terribly important had happened.

I had been a courier! *Moi*, Nicolette Bruiller. Could a nine-year-old save someone's life? I fantasized it to be so. Although *Papa* had sworn me to secrecy, I was dying to tell Miche of my Underground involvement. What good was it to be a hero if she didn't know it?

* * * * *

I hugged my doll—a constant nighttime companion ever since *Papa* let me choose her from the store window in Toulouse. Lying in bed next to my sisters—me and Miche on the outsides and Françoise in the middle, I struggled against the words of my good deed threatening to burst from my lips. Several times they almost babbled out to Miche, as I knew from her breathing she had not yet fallen asleep. Yet, *Papa* had entrusted me with something vitally important. Something grown up. The time had come for me to be too old for dolls. I gently caressed the face of my friend and kissed her before wrapping her in Françoise's free arm.

Papa's trust in me wrapped around my body. I fell asleep.

* * * * *

The next morning, I leapt out of bed and ran downstairs expecting *Papa* to inform me of the importance of my life-saving participation in *La Résistance Française.*

"*Bonjour*, Nicolette," he said.

"Good morning, *Papa*." I waited.

He sipped at his see-through coffee. *Maman* insisted he was fortunate to have it for many others did not have the means or access to coffee at all.

I continued to wait.

Papa winked at me.

I detected a conspiratorial smile.

For too long a time, nothing further came from *Papa*. That was it? That's all I got for all my valiant efforts?

* * * * *

We continued to live in the *château*, now absent of strange voices echoing in the night. Days ran into weeks into months into many more months and years. Routine without special guests to fill our time and space dulled our days but not our imaginations. We needed them to survive and paint color into this strange world.

Miche and I had enough fodder for inventiveness and play to last until we returned to our home in Paris.

* * * * *

It is the latter part of 1945. The war in Europe no longer rages.

I am now at the age of fourteen.

My family has returned to Paris. *Papa* still works as an industrialist, and continues to be successful. Although *Maman* has resumed her "life of luxury," she does not do so with presumption. She has devoted herself to making our community a kinder and more giving place to live. She welcomes outsiders and does not judge their circumstances.

Recently, *Papa* shared with me that the German who had befriended me was a defector from Hitler's army. His message divulged that the forest surrounding our house was filled with Nazi soldiers ready to advance on our mansion at the first sign of French Underground activity. The very evening I delivered the message was the night leaders of the French Resistance were to assemble in our secret passage for one of the most important meetings of the war. Of course, they never arrived thanks to those of us who valiantly linked arms with *La Résistance Française.*

"IN NO TIME IN NOWHERE"

October, 1940
Broken Wheel, Oklahoma

"Thilly Lily. Thilly Lily," Elmer sing-songed from the middle of the schoolyard.

Yesterday, Lily thought Elmer was lisping to make fun of her. That was before she saw his missing front tooth. Today she knew he was just plain taunting her because she was the new kid in school.

Tears brimmed Lily's eyes, threatening to give her away. She flung her head sideways, flipping her pigtails over her shoulders and marched past him. She tromped up the three sloping steps into Broken Wheel's one-room schoolhouse. Although it was mid-October, this was only her second day here in third grade. Lily wished she were back in Boston. Kids were a lot nicer there.

Lily's thoughts cartwheeled back to the day she overheard Pop tell Mom, "We've lost the house, and with gasoline now a whopping twenty cents a gallon, we can't afford to live in Boston. Besides, with my folks now gone on to their great reward, their farmhouse is sitting empty. Won't cost us a thing since the deed was left in my name."

Lily'd known right then Pop couldn't keep his promise to take her to see the new movie, *Pinocchio*. A quarter for each of their tickets wasn't going to happen. All right, so a stupid movie she sure could do without, but not her friends.

Mom'd told Pop—that day when he announced he was quitting his boxing career to take them to the farm where he'd grown up in Oklahoma—that no good would come of moving to the middle of *nowhere*. As far as Lily was concerned, fifth-graders Elmer and his buddy Doobie were proof of that.

Still, she'd rather be here with Pop than the other possibility. To Mom's argument, Pop had said, "It's either Oklahoma or the army for me. Hitler invaded Poland last year and it's just a matter of time before we get roped into war."

"That'll never happen." Mom planted her hands on her wide hips. "In fact, maybe if you enlisted we would have a steady income."

Pop had winced at that. Lily felt sorry for him. She knew how hard he tried to "bring home the bacon," as he called it. He'd come home from bouts in the ring with bumps, bruises, and black eyes. That part Lily didn't like at all, and she told him so.

"It's all part of the job," he'd said, thumbing his crooked nose. "If a guy can't take his lumps, then he's not worth his salt."

Well, now Lily would have to take her lumps. Wouldn't have to like them, but she would prove to Pop she was a fighter, too.

Another thing Pop said was, "Out here in the country you can be a kid—innocence and all—away from things happening in the rest of the world." Lily had never before seen Pop's face cloud over like that. Then, his face brightened when he added, "You're a smart whipper-snapper. You'll learn the ropes here in no time." Lily pictured him bobbing and weaving, punching the air as he spoke. She loved it when Pop sparred with her. It was their own special time together.

Ropes aren't the trouble, she thought as she hung her knitted sweater in the cloak closet behind the louvered blackboard doors. She turned to face the classroom and sucked in a chest full of courage before trudging toward the row of wood and cast iron desks. Though the back of her seat was connected to the front of Mary Lou's desk, Lily's was attached to the back of Elmer's seat. Every time he moved, Lily's desk jiggled. Elmer wiggled a lot, which made squiggles when she wrote in her tablet. The lines looked like the worms Elmer most likely had, which was why he wriggled so much.

That wasn't the worst of it. Elmer stunk up the space with all his wind breaking. She wasn't sure which was worse: Elmer's odors going up her nose, or his teases tramping through her ears into her brain.

Echoes of "Lil the pill," ricocheted in her head, along with "Lil hath a gill." Images of Elmer sucking his mouth into fish lips loomed. Then there was "Lil hath a bill," followed by Elmer's hands imitating a duck bill as he quacked. The only thing missing was him squatting to waddle.

Lily shook her head to shove away his cruel words. When she got the nerve up, she planned to beg Miss Kleidhoffer to move her. She didn't care where, just so long as it was outside the range of Elmer's toots and taunts. Besides, why should she, a third-grader, have to sit behind a front-row fifth-grader? Maybe she'd stay after school to beat erasers and ask her teacher then.

"Class, take your seats," Miss Kleidhoffer said.

Lily liked her teacher already. Yesterday she got after Elmer for filling his fountain pen from the Schaeffer's ink bottle he'd swiped from Miss K's desk. Lily rubbed at the dark indigo stain splatted in the shape of a dismembered butterfly on her freckled arm—compliments of Elmer the artist. He had to sit in the corner on a stool, which surprised Lily—not that the teacher sent him there, but that he could sit that long without wiggling off the perch or passing wind. Maybe that's what made the back of his neck so red—all that gas pressure.

I hope Elmer ends up in the corner again today. Lily crossed her fingers.

Miss K. walked past the wall of maps to the broom closet and squeaked the door open. Lily spied shelves lined with books of all sizes, red and green construction paper, and jars of white paste, which they'd made yesterday out of flour, salt, and water.

As soon as the teacher had her back to them, Elmer turned around and eyeballed Lily. Lily gasped at the too-close sight of another hole in his face.

"What happened? Someone knock one more of your teeth out?" Lily asked, surprised she'd even talked to him.

Elmer's ears turned red. Instead of answering Lily, he leaned across the aisle and asked his pal, Doobie, "Wonder what ol' Clodhopper ith gonna have uth do today?"

"Elmer, straighten up in your seat," Miss K. ordered.

Lily liked her teacher now more than she did a few minutes ago.

* * * * *

At recess, Lily made a beeline for the outhouse. Elmer headed her off at the pass. "Better be careful in there," he warned, hooking his thumbs in the straps of his dirty bib overalls. Sun reflected off the rooster tails of his red hair. Lily eyed him suspiciously. Doobie sniggered and lobbed rocks into the air.

In Boston, Lily's school had a flush toilet. This country school's little outhouse was disgusting. It had cracks and knotholes. How much privacy could there be with those? Yesterday, she'd tried not to look down the hole in the board's seat, but that didn't stop her from imagining what was down there.

"He'th juth waiting for fresh meat, ya know," Elmer said.

"Who is?" Lily was miffed at herself for speaking to him again.

"Thcat Rat," Elmer sneered.

"Thcat Rat?"

"No, Scat Rat. S, S-cat Rat," Doobie explained, coming to Elmer's rescue.

"What's a Scat Rat?" Lily asked, feeling dread scamper up her back.

"Well, ya got yer wood rat, yer pack rat, yer river rat, yer muthkrat, and yer thcat rat." Elmer grinned. "Ya know what thcat ith, don't ya?"

"You must think I'm stupid," Lily snorted. "Scat's when you tell somebody to get away."

Elmer and Doobie busted out in belly laughs. "Hoo-boy. Thath a good one." Elmer elbowed his sidekick.

"Yeah, ain't it though?" Doobie said more than asked, wrapping his arms around his ribs and hooting.

Elmer pushed his lips together and squished his eyes into a slit. "Theriouthly, though, thcat ith whath down the hole."

Lily felt her eyebrows close in on each other.

"Poop, ya dumbbell," Elmer explained. "Thtick with me, kid and I'll show ya the ropeth."

Lily felt her face heat up like Mom's black frying pan on the burner. She trounced off toward the outhouse, afraid she couldn't hold "it" anymore.

Elmer called after her, "Ol' Thcat Rat'll jump up and bite your fanny. Mark my wordth."

Laughter vibrated in Lily's ears. She jerked open the rickety wood-slatted door with a crescent notched out of it. When she pulled the door shut, she was glad for the sliver of light the little arc of a moon gave. She hooked the loop over the latch. Her mouth went dry and hairs prickled on her arms and neck. Her bladder was about to burst. She crossed her legs. She didn't dare turn around to face the hole. What if what Elmer said was true? Yesterday when she was in here, she thought she'd heard something swimming around down there. Lily shuddered at the thought of Scat Rat ready to fly out of the deep, dark pit and sink his pointy teeth into her. Staying only as long as it would take to convince Elmer she had done her business, she clenched her fist, and repeated, "I don't have to go. I don't have to go." Trying to appear as casual as possible, she unlooped the latch and stepped out. It took every ounce of courage she didn't have to run as far away from Scat Rat as she could.

Lily knew Elmer was watching. She ambled in a wide arc around him and his buddies playing marbles over to where Mary Lou and another girl played hopscotch. Back in Boston, she'd used chalk to draw connecting boxes on sidewalks. Mary Lou's squares were scratched on the ground. Lily had used a bean bag. Mary Lou tossed a flat rock onto the dirt squares.

"Wanna play?" Mary Lou asked.

"Sure," Lily said. She was good at hopping from one square to the next without stepping on the lines. On the first hop, Lily came down on one foot. A trickle of warmth seeped into her panties. Lily felt Elmer's eyes still on her. She looked around for a different activity. A gaggle of girls were jumping rope. *Even worse.*

From the top step of the schoolhouse, the teacher rang the hand bell. Clang-a-lang. Clang-a-ling. Recess was over. *Saved by the bell!* Could she make it 'til noon?

The rest of the morning Lily fidgeted in her seat, trying as she might to figure out how to solve her problem. She wished she hadn't downed so much apple cider for breakfast. Tomorrow she'd be sure to not drink anything before coming to school. A dry mouth was better than wet pants. That was tomorrow. She still had to deal with today.

She looked at the Regulator clock hanging on the wall above Miss K's desk. Its pendulum swung back and forth, back and forth, ticking away the few minutes left until noon when she would have to do something—or burst.

I wonder if I can sneak away from everybody into the bushes out back. Just the thought of the squat to take care of matters made her blush. *I hate Elmer for making me even think such things!* She stared at the back of his ugly head.

Elmer turned around and stuck out his tongue. Or maybe he couldn't stop it from poking out that gigantic hole between his teeth that were still in his mouth.

"All right, class. That will be all until after you eat." Miss K. closed *The Happy Grammar* primer.

Lily was the first up and out of her seat. She couldn't wait another second. To heck with ol' Scat Rat. If he wanted to bite her butt that bad, he'd have to be fast because she'd be faster. After running out the door and down the steps and across the yard, Lily whipped the outhouse door open. She hovered over the hole in the seat. Relief at last! Not taking time to wipe with a sheet from the Sears and Roebuck catalogue, she sprang from the outhouse. Without being bitten by ol' Scat Rat, even if his beady little eyes were watching.

*****

That night, Scat Rat barged into Lily's bedroom. His pointy nose was wet against her cheek. His razor teeth gnawed her ear. His fur grazed her skin, chilling her paralyzed body. There was no getting away from him. His rancid breath was hot against her face. Lily couldn't breathe. She was falling down the hole. Her fingernails clawed at the edge of the circle in the wooden toilet seat. A bright light beamed in through the crescent moon slit. The door flew open. Elmer leapt in, grabbed her arms and pulled her from the outhouse hole—to the gaping, toothless hole in his head.

"NO! NO!" Wrestling to free herself from his grip, Lily flailed and wailed. Her fingers brushed against something and wrapped around it. A rope. It was a rope! Grabbing hold with the other hand, she pulled for all she was worth, pulling away from the terror of Elmer's hold on her.

"Lily. Lily, wake up."

From an abyss, Lily hauled herself up, up, and out. Through the crusty sleep in her eyes, she could barely make out her mother's disheveled hair. Her hands relaxed, letting go of the belt of Mom's chenille bathrobe.

"You're having a bad dream," Mom said, smoothing hair from Lily's sweaty face.

Pop appeared at the threshold, his body filling the doorway. "What's going on?" He raked fingers through his thick, black hair. Lily almost laughed at the way it stuck straight up until it reminded her of Elmer's rooster tails.

Pop sauntered to the end of her bed and plopped down.

Lily explained about the Scat Rat.

A chuckle started in Pop's chest, rumbled around a bit before boiling up his throat and bursting from his mouth in a guffaw. When he quieted down, he shook his head. "Boys're still up to that ol' trick, eh?" He tousled her hair. "Ol' Elmer sounds like the kind you don't want to make enemies with."

Pop was usually right about things, but Lily wasn't so sure about this.

* * * * *

The next morning, Lily skipped onto the playground, wearing the same pink-checkered dress she'd worn all week. She only had that one, so she had to make sure she didn't get it dirty. Well, she did have a Sunday-go-to-meeting dress, but she had to save it for that one day.

"Well now, if it ithn't Thilly Lily Thcat Rat Thcaredy Cat," Elmer teased.

Without so much as a blink of a gnat's eye, Lily shot back, "The only rat around here is you." She sniffed at him, scrunched her nose and pinched her nostrils together between her finger and thumb, and added, "Elmer-Scat-In-Your-Pants." Lily marched right past him and a chuckling Doobie—who had taken a sharp elbow to the ribs. She plopped onto the schoolhouse steps and straightened the skirt of her cotton dress. Retying her saddle shoelaces, she knew Pop was right, she'd learned the ropes in no time

Now she could focus on the real problem. She missed her Boston friends more than she let on. She would never see them again. Tears pooled in her eyes. She swiped away the moisture and squared her shoulders. She'd rather face Elmer than the embarrassment of being a bawl baby.

Her eyes searched the school yard. Children ages five through twelve littered the grounds. A couple of first-grade girls teeter-tottered on a plank, their skirts billowing out on the way down. A bigger kid attempted to reach the sky on a tire swing hanging from an oak tree.

I'm gonna make new friends here. She raised her hand and waved. "Hi, Mary Lou. Want to play jacks?" Lily held up a bag and drew out a little, red, rubber ball.

Mary Lou motioned to a spot in the yard. "The ground here is nice and hard." Lily jumped up to join her. After they sat down. Lily let Mary Lou go first.

"Elmer don't got no mom," Mary Lou said.

"Elmer doesn't have a mom?" Lily asked, not sure she heard right.

"That's what I said."

"Why?"

"His mom died last year from berculosis, or anthrax, or something horrible."

A twinge of sympathy poked Lily.

Mary Lou bounced the ball and scooped up a jack. "When his dad gets drunk, he belts Elmer around. S'how he lost his teeth." She bounced the ball again, this time scooping up two jacks. Then three. Before long she had them all in her hand. "Your turn," Mary Lou said, handing them over.

Lily didn't know what to say. Her dad would never hit her. And she had her mom. Something the size of the ball in her hand lumped up in her throat.

Without warning, a billy goat charged onto the playground. It lowered its head and rammed the boy on the swing. The tire twisted round and round. The boy wrapped his arms around the rubber and stuck his feet straight out. On the next swivel, they plowed into the goat's head knocking him away. The billy stampeded toward the ring of marble players. They scattered. The goat lowered his horns and ran for the jump-ropers, who quickly flung the rope in the air and made for the schoolhouse steps.

Lily could hardly believe what she was seeing, and for sure couldn't move. Especially when the goat eyeballed her sitting on the ground, then headed straight for her. She screamed but couldn't get up. Her shoes only skidded in the dirt.

The beast snorted and picked up speed.

Lily clamped her hands over her eyes, bracing herself. When the hit didn't come, she peeked out between the slit in her fingers.

Elmer had lassoed the goat with the jump rope and pulled with all his might. His face was red and sweaty. The brute turned on him and charged. Elmer hunkered down and held his ground. A second before the billy made contact, Elmer ducked aside.

Like Lily had seen her dad do in the ring.

Elmer yanked on the rope and the goat's feet went out from underneath him. Elmer pounced on top of him and wrapped the end of the cord around the animal's legs. The goat bleated and bellowed.

Standing up and dusting himself off, Elmer turned to Lily. "Didn't I tell ya I'd show ya the ropeth?" He smiled at her, flashing what teeth he had.

At once, the hole in Elmer's head somehow had character.

"Thanks." Lily flashed a smile of her own.

Her new friend's face turned as red as his hair.

Pop would be glad to hear that she'd made friends in no time in Nowhere.

"DEAR DAD"

Dekator, Alabama
October 1, 1941

Dear Dad,
I wanted to write this letter myself but so far they don't teach nothing in second grade. How's a guy gonna write a letter if all he can spell is: See, Dick, Jane, Spot, and run— the same hogwash they tried pushing off on us in first grade. As you can see, my vocabulary is getting bigger. Hogwash— Grandma taught me that word. Pretty nifty, huh? It sure comes in handy. Except for when I said that word to Mom's boss when he called me a scrawny little runt.

Aunt Mabel said as long as she has to watch me while Grandma's taking a nap and Mom's working down at Milo's Grocery, she'd type while I talk. I'm helping her out 'cause she needs practice on her Royal typewriter. She's s'posed to be putting everything down just like I say. I made her say the "stick a needle in my eye" deal. She said that's a no-lie oath, but isn't that what a promise is, Dad? I gotta be sure Aunt Mabel don't change my words and that you know this letter is really from me.

"Fine, Scooter, you made your point. Needle . . . point. Get it?" Aunt Mabel asked. She thinks she's funny. But not as funny as her belly bobbing when she laughs. She didn't want to write any of this, but I made her include it so you can see what's really going on around here.

I'm gonna ask you when you get home if she really wrote about her belly 'cause I'm not sure she put that in here. Her lips pruned up about her belly. I'm gonna ask you about the pruned lips, too.

Thanks for the pictures of you and your ship. The U.S.S. Arizona sure is big. I showed them to Boomer. His dad's in the Marines. Boomer called you a limey sea-dog. I told him his dad was slimey. He said you were a gob. I punched him one in the gut. He decked me, but I don't got no regrets that I stood up for you. I'm just letting you know I'm holding up to being the man in the house while you're in the Navy.

I gotta go. Aunt Mabel says her fingers are seizing up.
Love,
Scooter

* * * * *

October 15, 1941

Dear Dad,

Thanks for letting me know Aunt Mabel put it in my letter about her belly and lips.

Are there really pearls in your harbor? Boomer said there ain't none, that that's just an old wives' tale. I told him wives don't have tails. He called me stupid. Just when I was gonna tell him he is a dimwit, Susie Shwartz elbowed in. I told her to mind her own beeswax. Boomer's afraid of her brother Butch 'cause he punched Boomer's cousin's lights out last week.

Boomer's been blabbing around that Susie's sweet on me. Don't you just hate girls, Dad?
Love,
Scooter

* * * * *

October 22, 1941

Dear Dad,

Aunt Mabel said if I wipe the sandman's sleep out of my eyes, I won't never be able to get back to sleep? Is that true?

Gosh oh gee, how's a fella to know stuff with just women around? I miss you, Dad. I wish you were here so I could ask you important questions. It's awful hard being the man of the house. Women are always trying to take over. You're lucky being on the ship with all those men.

Unless you have a nincompoop like Boomer around. He called me Scooter, schmooter and yelled all over the playground that I never learned to walk, so I scoot like a baby.

Dad, when you write back, I'm going by my real name now.
Love,
Junior

* * * * *

November 7, 1941

Dear Dad,

I just got your letter ten minutes ago. Thanks for calling me Junior.

I told Mom she sure is getting fat. She laughed, then she told me a secret. I asked if Dad knew. She laughed again. Did you know she's gonna have a baby?

See, that's why I need you here. Women are doing all these things on their own. Making decisions. Calling the shots. Nobody asks me nothing. They just tell me what to do.

I gotta go now to take out the trash.

Love,

Junior

* * * * *

November 23, 1941

Dear Dad,

Thanksgiving is gonna be lonely without you. I hope the U.S.S. Arizona can get enough turkeys to feed all you guys. Do they even grow turkeys in Hawaii?

When do you get to ship out to sea? I don't think I would like being docked. Aunt Mabel said she got docked yesterday for being late to work. She's swell for writing my letters, but she's a little slow, if you get my drift.

Sheesh. What'd I say? Criminee, now she won't write any more.

Love,

Junior

* * * * *

November 27, 1941

Dear Dad,

I told Grandma as man of the house, I need to make some moolah 'cause chores don't pay nothing. She snapped her fingers and said she had just the opportunity for me. Quick cash, she said.

There's this Pillsbury Thrift Star Contest. I'll win $3,000.00 in the grand prize. Or, if I don't get that one, first prize is still $500.00! All I have to do is say in thirty-five words or less, "It pays to buy Pillsbury's Best Flour because . . ." The only catch is I have to send it in with a Pillsbury Star from a bag of flour—Pillsbury, wouldn't you just know? They always get you some way, huh?

So, here was my sentence: "It pays to buy Pillsbury's Best Flour because without it Mom couldn't make my birthday cake." That was my first shot. I counted the words Aunt Mabel typed, and I only used eight of my own words (after the because)—nine if they're gonna count couldn't as two. I figured I might get deducted for such a short sentence. They want you to butter them up good, so I added on to it. Here is my final prize-winning sentence: "It pays to buy Pillsbury's Best Flour because without it Mom could not make my birthday cake and how can I be the man of the house if I don't feel older, not to mention that it keeps you guys in business." That's thirty-four words, but I left a little slack in case they count birthday as two words and don't as two.

Now Aunt Mabel says I have to count "It pays to buy Pillsbury's Best Flour because . . ." If that's the case, then I have to start over and cut out my best work.

Grandma got the contest out of a magazine. In it I saw a brand new Studebaker Champion that gets 29.19 miles per gallon. It sells for $660.00. But if I win the grand prize, I'm buying Mom the Packard 120 for $1,038.00. That'll leave plenty for a crib. As you can see, my math is getting good.

Mom hasn't gone to work for a while 'cause the baby is coming next week. She says it will be a nice welcome home bundle when you are here on your Christmas leave.

See you soon. I can hardly wait—for you *and* the $3,000.00.
Love,
Junior

* * * * *

December 7, 1941

Dear Dad,

You ain't gonna believe this. After I been waiting at the mailbox all week, come to find out that dumb Pillsbury Contest came out of an old magazine. What's the point of Grandma keeping an April, 1940 issue of *Life* laying around the house? What a waste of three pennies for a stupid stamp. Actually, six cents. I sent off two entries. I figured it didn't hurt to double my chances.

That's not even the bad news. Even worse is, guess what? Mom had a baby girl last night. It didn't do us no good to hold out for a boy, did it? It's a good thing you have me and I have you. Guess we'll have to settle for two men in the house. When you get home, we'll stick together. Even if we'll be outnumbered.

Aunt Mabel's trying to hurry me up to get to church. Why should I go? God didn't give me a brother, even after I hounded Him for one.

I gotta turn down the radio. The guy on it is yelling about Japanese and Pearl Harbor where you're at. Something's hap

"BROTHER'S KEEPER"

November, 1942
Powderville, Montana

William Thomas Jennings perched on the lip of the grave, its jaws at the ready to swallow his father. Willie wrestled against tears threatening to leak from his eyes. As always, his will won out. He had to be strong, just as he was almost eleven years ago when he stood in this same spot. That day, they buried his mother and his stillborn sister. That day, at five years of age, Willie saw his father withdraw into his own world. Willie watched his brother Tommy sob uncontrollably. Even as a kindergartner then, Willie would not allow himself to weaken.

Now, Pa's coffin descended into the open pit.

Willie raised his eyes to study his brother. Tommy—although two years older—had always depended on him. At school, Willie had often stepped in to protect his brother who, townswomen said, had his mother's gentle character and fragile frame.

Ma. Willie shifted his eyes to the adjacent grassy, almost-indistinct mound, then to its headstone. *Eugenia Mae Jennings. May 1, 1901—April 8, 1931.*

Her laughter rolled up from a dim recess of his mind and filled his ears. He squeezed his palm as if her dainty fingers were there. From his memory, he drew a breath of that year's spring air wafting around right in this same place. The fragrance of those cherry blossoms reminded him of how he had snuggled into Ma's bosom, into the scent of her.

A flutter of crows' wings in a nearby elm wrenched him from his comfort. He read the next line on Ma's marker: *Lissie Eugenia Jennings. April 8, 1931.* Willie wondered if his sister, dead at birth, now resting in Ma's arms, gave Ma comfort.

Because a part of Pa went to that grave with them that day, Willie took on the task of tending to Tommy—to see that he always had his blanket, to comfort him in his childhood illness. Doctors never pinpointed what caused Tommy to be sick, but he eventually outgrew whatever it was.

Willie took pride in teaching Tommy how to feed the chickens and gather eggs, just as Ma had taught him. After a couple of years, they added milking cows to their daily routine. As they grew, throwing hay bales and driving the International tractor consumed their springs, summers, and falls. However, Willie never insisted Tommy help with butchering. Whether it be killing chickens or slaughtering hogs, Tommy would puke his guts out at the sight of blood.

Tommy was more into rescuing wounded animals. Like the baby bunny he found near death. Tommy nursed it back to health. For as long as it lived, it followed Tommy everywhere. In the barnyard, through the house, to bed. Didn't matter.

By the time Willie reached ten, he had surpassed Tommy in size, both in height and build. Soon, strangers surmised Willie was the older brother. Willie felt older, acted older.

Today, now that Pa was gone, it was just he and Tommy— if he didn't count Ma's sister in Cincinnati, whom they hadn't seen since Ma's funeral.

Willie couldn't think about that now. His shoulders slumped at the burden of Pa's indebtedness. The bank owned the ranch and all of the equipment. What would they do now? He didn't have a plan.

* * * * *

Thomas William Jennings—Tommy—fixed his eyes on the clods thumping onto Pa's coffin. His hand brushed against an envelope in the side pocket of his tattered, oversized suit coat. Uncle Sam's letter, which had come the day before the tractor tipped over and crushed Pa, sucked the life out of Tommy.

Yellow-belly. Fraidy-cat. Elementary-school-classmate taunts from years past rang in his ears. He felt Willie's eyes on him, yet he couldn't look up. Willie—his protector, his rescuer. How could Willie save him from this?

* * * * *

"Foreclosure's tomorrow." Willie tugged Pa's WWI Navy sea bag out of the closet. "This'll hold all our clothes."

Tommy sagged onto the bed.

Willie tugged open a dresser drawer. From the corner of his eye, he noticed Tommy's hesitation. "Why aren't you packing?"

Tommy hauled an envelope from his overalls and thrust it at Willie.

"What's this?" From the return address, Willie instantly grasped the magnitude of the moment. "When'd you get this?"

"Day before Pa died."

"How come you didn't tell me?"

Tommy shrugged. "Didn't want to worry you."

Willie pulled out the letter, read. His chest tightened. "Tomorrow. You gotta report tomorrow!"

Tommy scratched his head. "What am I going to do, Willie?"

Willie knew his brother would never survive. Even without a war waging in Europe. "Give me a minute, will you?" He stared at himself in the dresser mirror. Behind him sat Tommy. The difference between their statures, their demeanors, shouted the only answer.

Willie knocked the cowboy hat off Tommy's head, tossed it onto the bedpost. He did the same with his own Stetson—a prize he'd won in a calf roping contest. "Won't be wearing these where we're going," he said.

* * * * *

From this day on he was no longer Thomas William Jennings. He was William Thomas Jennings, the sixteen year-old. His brother was now supposedly eighteen, going off to war. Guilt and relief duked it out inside him. He would have to repeat all of his junior and senior years. School he could survive—even thrive in. The Army he could not.

But could he live with it if Willie died in the war?

* * * * *

Relief and worry whirled around Willie as he stood in line for his physical. Could he pull off being Thomas William Jennings, an eighteen-year-old? In order to avoid not responding to his brother's name, and the "Tommy" image it evoked in his mind, Willie had talked Tommy into keeping their own names, as nicknames. It sounded confusing, but they would convince Aunt Verna they went by their middle names. The Army shouldn't be a problem, since they tagged a guy by his last name.

So, even though he was now Thomas William Jennings on paper, he would still be "Willie." He liked the idea of being the older brother. It felt right.

"Jennings!"

The call to step forward sent a thrill through him. The poking and probing into previously untouched parts of his body did not.

Everything whizzed by after that. Even his hair, toppling in brown clumps over his face. When he filled in the lines of his several-thousand-dollar's worth of government life insurance policy, he put down the fountain pen and paused. He hadn't anticipated this crinkle in the crunch. Finally, beside beneficiary, he scrawled William Thomas Jennings. He chuckled at the irony of paying himself to die.

* * * * *

"Willie!" Aunt Verna's high-pitched voice rose above the locomotive's shrill cry as she held up a very old black-and-white photograph, looking at it, then at him stepping off the train.

Tommy hefted the sea bag over his shoulder as he approached his aunt. When within arm's length, he stated, "Tommy."

His aunt's smile curved, questioning.

"I go by my middle name."

"Uh, well, then. You look just like your mother; bless her heart. Don't get me started on her passing. You look emaciated. First thing, I'll fatten you up. Eugenia would never forgive me

59

if I let you waste away. Bless her heart. Wait 'til you see what I've done to fix up your room. Painted it blue and sewed a bedspread and curtains to match. Never mind they're made out of flour sacks; they took the blue dye well. Mercy me, look at your britches. They just hang on you." She regarded his western shirt and cowboy boots, then pursed her lips while pointing to his feet. "Boys here don't wear those. I'll not have anyone poking fun of the way you dress. If it's two things I can do for your sweet mama it's to feed and clothe you. I'm quite a seamstress, you know. Did you wear those things I sent over the years? I'll whip you up some fancy duds. Won't all the young ladies just swarm around you when they see how handsome you are? Sorry I couldn't make it to your Pa's funeral, but, uh, well, I'm just so busy working and minding my own business—"

Tommy tuned her out and wondered if he and Willie had done the right thing.

* * * * *

Boot camp wasn't as bad as Willie had heard. It had bulked up his muscles even more and added to his endurance. He could run three miles without breaking a sweat, could pump out one-hundred pushups in no time, and could load, reload, dismantle and reassemble his M1 rifle blindfolded. The few months afterwards, waiting on base for orders to ship out, was the hard part. Now, a buck private making $1.62 a day, he was finally deployed into action, along with his rifle platoon of 192 comrades—although none of them knew where they were headed due to classified information.

For the umpteenth time Willie reached for the chain around his neck, pulled out his dog tags and read the inscription: Thomas William Jennings, 39229300, A, P

The first number three in his serial number indicated he was drafted. Had he enlisted or volunteered, it would have been a one. The A designated his blood type. He hoped they would never need that information. P showed he was Protestant, although he hadn't been inside a church since Ma's funeral. Pa had made sure of that.

The two sets of identical tags were a constant reminder of his mortality.

If it comes to that, at least I will have spared Tommy's life.

* * * * *

Upon their arrival "home," Aunt Verna threw her arms around Tommy and pulled him into her ample chest. She kissed his neck. The fragrance of cherry blossoms wafted into Tommy's nostrils. The scent of it triggered something within him. From somewhere in the recess of his memory his mother was comforting him. Tears sprang to his eyes. He did not budge from his aunt's embrace.

Finally, she released her hold and reached behind the top button of her dress. She pulled out a handkerchief, shook it out, and dabbed her eyes. "Now don't get me to blubbering or I'll be of no good to you." She led him through the house to his bedroom, talking non-stop.

At supper that evening, Tommy got a big serving of his aunt's hospitality and household management: "Tommy, eat everything on your plate. As a nurse, I know full well how important that is."

Thereafter, Aunt V hounded him at breakfast, dinner, and supper. Upon him slicking up every last morsel, she would scoop more onto his platter. After six months, when he still hadn't gained any weight, she pronounced, "You've got worms!"

She dragged him to her employer—a local doctor. When it hadn't proved to be worms, she resorted to pumping him full of a questionable substance. She'd ripped a page from the back of a magazine and produced a picture of a skeletal man beside Charles Atlas. The advertisement promised to turn any weakling into a hulk of a man. For the past month Tommy had been forced to down the foul tasting tonic.

He wondered how Willie was faring on K rations. Or C rations. He wasn't sure of the difference between the two.

* * * * *

Now, two years later, Willie's back ached. His arms screamed. His legs felt like fence posts. For hours he and Jake had hacked away at the frozen ground fortified by stones and tree roots. The twenty-eight-inch entrenching tool in his hands proved practically useless in digging a foxhole. Thirty minutes of shoveling gained a mere few inches of headway. Despite the freezing wind and snow, perspiration drizzled down Willie's back. As much as he hated this work's assault on his body, he dreaded even more what would happen to the sweat when he stopped. Long-johns offered little insulation at that point.

Willie straightened to massage his muscles. Removing his wool gloves, he unwelded his fingers from their handle-molded position. He crooked his neck, rotated it from side to side, arched his spine. His eyes swept 180 degrees over their encampment. He and Jake had made a bigger dent in the mandatory three-by-eight-foot hole than others in their infantry platoon. Foxholes were to be twenty feet apart, two riflemen per hole.

Back home he'd dug more postholes than he cared to count. But that was in the spring or summer for fences in Montana. This was frozen dirt, deep in a German forest. Nonetheless, his efforts were for freedom—Tommy's freedom. Willie tried to convince himself that he had never *not* been free, and wondered if truly he had never been shackled by fear. He stopped digging. However, if he didn't get back to work he could be confined forever in a box.

"Jennings!"

The voice startled him to attention. "Yes, sir, Sarge."

"This might help move things along." Sarge handed him an axe.

The tool infused Willie with new energy.

By nightfall, he and Jake collapsed into their foxhole. They'd accomplished their mission of three feet deep but had only been able to carve out three feet of length. It would have to do. Out of the wind, Willie felt some reprieve as he dug into his pack and pulled out K rations. Beneath the green outer wrapping, a plain tan, waxed box promised sustenance. Tonight's canned meatloaf, biscuit, and hard candy would hit the spot. As would the toilet paper. This meant Willie had to climb out of the foxhole into the wind to the straddle trench.

He eyeballed the distance to it from their foxhole. "Guess I shouldn't complain about having to go so far," he said to Jake, sniffing the air. "But even from here, the fragrance isn't too pleasant."

He hoisted himself out of the hole and was back in ten twitches of a mule's whisker. He settled in for first watch. Two hours on, then four hours sleep. Welcome sleep—even if in a hole not a whole lot unlike the ones where his Ma, sister, and Pa rested.

* * * * *

Even though two years had already passed, Aunt V could no longer handle his nickname. "Tommy is no name for an eighteen-year-old," she said, setting her jaw and plunking her hands on her plump hips. "It's well past time you started dating, so you've got to present yourself with the right allure. Is that the word I want to use? Well, you know what I mean. From now on you'll be either Thomas or Tom. Which will it be?"

Tommy smiled. If she only knew how old he really was. Her idea wasn't bad, though. Now that Willie wasn't around, he didn't feel so little, so vulnerable. Bossy Aunt Verna had jolted him out of his cocoon. Even though he wished he were back on the farm, given the situation, living with Aunt V wasn't all that bad. Cincinnati High offered opportunities not available in podunk Powderville. Such as playing the oboe. He hadn't been able to join band because of all the chores he and Willie had shared.

Tommy . . . Tom realized music gave him wings. Every afternoon in band he flew to the rafters, in his heart and mind. And not just at school. Aunt V had placed a General Electric radio in his room. Lena Horne lifted him right out of his chair. He could only aspire to such loftiness. But he had a start— Aunt V had gotten him into the Northlake Baptist Church choir.

Church. After Ma died, Pa had refused to let them go. Recently, on Sundays, Tom heard things that made him want to believe God loved him. Still, how could a loving God let his ma and sister die so young? How could God let a tractor crush Pa to death? However confused, Tom didn't stop praying for Willie.

The Christmas Cantata was next week, and Tom had landed the tenor soloist part. All of a sudden, Carol Carson made a point to talk to him after practice. She didn't have a lead role, but did have a sweet voice. Tonight he planned to ask her to the movies on Saturday night. He sure would like to take her in Aunt V's Packard, a gas guzzler that would probably burn up his aunt's ration cards. So he didn't dare ask.

Even with rations, life was good, and getting better all the time.

* * * * *

For Willie, four days passed without more than a few minutes of stolen sleep. Even when it came upon him, it afforded little rest. Cold was a constant companion. Wind-driven ice stung his face and cut with razor-blade ferocity. His fingers, without sensation for three days, failed him in the buttoning of his field jacket. His thin, wool socks granted no defense against frostbite. He would welcome *dry*, socks, wool or not. As snow melted, the bottom of the foxhole filled with mud and slush. His boots weren't waterproof. What idiot had designed them? Even more to the point, what idiot officer had requisitioned them? Obviously a General who had never been wet and icy to the bones on the front line.

Initially, the slight mound of dirt he and Jake had formed in the middle of their tiny foxhole to stand on provided some respite from slush but hadn't warded off injury to their feet. Willie's toes were numb and purple. His mouth felt stuffed with wool. Without water for brushing teeth, his stinky breath snaked up his nostrils and stung his eyes. He had tried catching snow in his metal helmet, but the melting process was long and arduous, and netted more cold than help.

The powdered coffee in their K rats was a good idea—if he'd had hot water. Willie was grateful for the sugar tablets, however, that melted on his tongue. Cigarettes, he used to barter for t.p.

Wonder if Tommy's taken to smoking? Probably not. *His lungs couldn't take it.*

*****

Something had happened tonight to Tom that he couldn't explain. For the first time ever, he felt peace . . . and free. It had happened right in the middle of his song, at the realization of the Christmas message. Something else had happened as well. His performance had garnered a standing ovation. At first shy over the adulation, he quickly came to embrace—not so much the attention—but the confirmation of his calling in life.

This December day marked yet another milestone—his first kiss.

Carol had not left his side after the Cantata. In the church basement during refreshments, she had made it known to all the other girls—while patting her hand on his Aunt-V-made-brand-new-green shirt—that he was with *her*. Aunt V had been miffed at Carol's possessiveness, but Tom rather liked the idea of Carol being *his* girl.

"No good comes from a floozy," his aunt said when they piled into the Packard.

Tom was embarrassed at her catching him kissing Carol behind the church. "She's not a floozy. I kissed her first."

"Well, any girl that would allow a young man to take her behind the building in the first place can't have too many scruples. Why, when I was a young *lady* I never would have even *dreamed* of such a thing."

Probably why she's an old maid.

"Even at that, having a girlfriend does put a sparkle in your eyes. Your new shirt provided just the allure I intended." Aunt V winked at him.

She rattled on but Tom quit listening. He'd seen the way she made calf eyes at the school bus driver, widower Dick Haney. Truth be told, Mr. Haney didn't seem to mind the fact that Aunt V dominated conversations in the church basement after Sunday services. He sure hadn't minded Aunt V's cherry pies and honey biscuits she foisted on him to take home. Nobody called her on her lie that she had so much food she didn't know what to do with it, so why not put it to good use? Some women raised their eyes and questioned where Aunt V got all the sugar to bake. Tom knew his aunt had no sugar. She was just creative with honey and fruit she boiled down from her orchard into a sweet concentrate.

Although a domineering ratchet jaw, Aunt V had wormed her way into Tom's heart. He knew she wanted only the best for him and loved him as the son she'd never had. He almost felt guilty at the lie he was living right under her roof. If he ever told her the truth, would she feel she had been played for a fool? He'd come close once to being found out when she commented on the mole on the back of his neck.

"I recall a mole on Thomas' neck right in that very same spot. I noticed it when he bent his head as Eugenia's coffin was lowered." Aunt V squinted her eyes. "Or was it Willie?" She shook her head. "When did you two switch names? What would your Mama think of her sons taking on their middle names?" She clucked her tongue, adding, "Leaving two young boys behind to fend for themselves. Why, she'd roll over in her grave if she knew your Pa never remarried. Goodness sakes, trying to raise little boys by himself with all that farm work. I don't know what he was thinking." She bit her lip. "I wanted so badly to bring you boys here, but your father wouldn't hear of it." She paused, pressed her palms to her cheeks. "I simply couldn't leave my Director of Nursing job. And your father . . . well, we wouldn't have gotten along. I hope you don't hold it against me for not coming to take care of you."

Tom closed his eyes and relived Carol's kiss.

* * * * *

Before dawn broke, a rumble overhead jarred Willie out of a dream. As he emerged from the first deep moment of sleep he'd had in days, he wondered if he'd imagined the noise. Eerie silence permeated the air. Then a great explosion engulfed the area.

"V-1 buzz bomb," Jake shouted.

Light burst on the horizon, revealing oncoming tanks.

"Our tanks!"

Within seconds the foreboding roar of airplanes, dozens of them, howled overhead.

"German Luftwaffe!"

Panzer Faust rockets screamed from the sky, knocking out one American tank, then another. The ground shook.

Fully awake, adrenalin coursed through Willie's body. Scrambling to get his blood circulating, he stomped his feet and blew on his fingers. If he was to do any damage, he'd have to recoup feeling in his hands. Judging from the ice on his eyebrows and the frozen mud on the foxhole floor, he figured the temperature to be in the twenties. As he jounced his body into firing position, he wished he'd visited the straddle trench before retiring after his watch. Diarrhea had joined the cold in becoming every soldier's worst enemy.

Diarrhea and trench foot are the least of my worries now.

A second V-1 exploded, this time much nearer. In the resulting light, he saw mounds approaching. *Jerries!* He opened up his semiautomatic rifle, firing off thirty-four rounds in the next minute.

"Hold it! Hold on!" Jake hollered above the din. "Those're dirt mounds, Jennings. Not Krauts."

Engines growled across the sky, the sound different from the first flock of planes.

"B-17s. Ours!"

The good news was short-lived. Directly behind the American planes a heavy barrage of enemy artillery and rockets assaulted American front lines. The deafening noise obliterated communication from foxhole to foxhole. The battle raged throughout the day and into the night.

By the third day, the platoon was out of ammunition, all communications severed. What had happened to their commander? Frozen, dead bodies littered the field. Shells continued to drop from the sky with the roar of a tornado.

With not even a grenade left in his arsenal, Willie squatted at the bottom of his foxhole. He rummaged in his pack. He pulled out a ballpoint pen and a K rat wrapper, turning it over to print a final message. Even with frozen fingers he was able to scrawl a few words.

> Dear Tommy,
> Always remember, this was my choice.
> Love forever,
> Willie

After rereading the note, he folded it into fourths and tucked it into his breast pocket. He felt sick to his stomach.

Fear slithered through him, wrapping tentacles around his heart, his mind.

* * * * *

Tom bolted upright in the dark, saturated with sweat. His heart pounding, his mouth dry, he threw off the mound of suffocating blankets.

Willie! Something's happened to Willie!

Clutching his stomach and forcing back bile threatening to propel from his guts, he cried, "God, don't let Willie die. Please. Protect him and bring him home safe and sound."

Easing onto his pillow, Tom continued to pray for his brother. Soon, reassurance that God would answer his prayers filled him with peace—the same peace he'd come to know a few nights ago during the Cantata. With this peace had also come freedom. It didn't make sense, however. How could freedom be gained by giving his life to Christ? It was more than he could fathom. Nonetheless, it was more real than anything he'd ever known. For the first time in his life, he did not feel buried by fear and dread.

Better get some sleep. Got a long bus ride tomorrow.

Tom drifted off to sleep thinking of Carol and how much fun they would have together at the game.

* * * * *

The screaming meemies shrieked overhead. The sky opened like a floodgate spilling German rockets.

Coward.

The self-imposed accusation stuck like a bone in Willie's craw. The truth of the word *coward* left him debilitated. He wasn't ready to die. He didn't want to die. For all his outward bravado, he realized he'd lied to himself . . . to Tommy.

Truth was, when his mother died, Willie hadn't allowed himself to cry. But it had nothing to do with courage. He now realized it was because if he hadn't been strong, he would have gone to the grave with Ma. Fear had been his motivating force all along.

"Jennings! Get your head out of the clouds. Move out." Jake pounded a fist on Willie's helmet.

Dazed with dread, Willie crawled out of the foxhole. A flash ripped through the air, followed by a deafening sound. Flying fragments of an exploding grenade found their mark.

Sheering pain slashed open a sea of red. Blackness swallowed Willie.

* * * * *

Tom awoke, all excited. He'd gotten special permission to ride with the basketball team to a pre-league scrimmage. Most of the team's parents had donated gasoline coupons to fill the bus with petrol so the teens could have a sneak peek at their rival. Carol would meet him there. He quickly threw on Aunt V's newest creation—a blue, tailored shirt. Fitting gold cufflinks into the slits, he liked the starched crispness of the sleeves. Slicking his hair back, he whistled his way through the rest of his morning ritual.

After a bacon-and-egg breakfast with marmalade-slathered toast—no butter—he dashed out of the house. "See you later, Aunt V," he called over his shoulder. "Don't know what time we'll be back."

"Just a minute, young man."

Tom skidded to a halt. *Uh oh. What did I do? Or didn't do?*

"Take these to Mr. Haney." Aunt V thrust a package at him.

"Mmm. Snickerdoodles."

"Don't you dare eat a one of these. There are plenty in the kitchen for you when you get home—"

"I love you," he said, cutting her off. Grabbing the bundle, he ran down the sidewalk before she could grab him into a hug and make him late.

When he arrived at the school, the bus was fired up, black exhaust rolling from its tailpipe. The back seats already filled, he took a place by the window right behind Mr. Haney.

The bus driver thumped his chest with the side of his fist. "I woke up with a bit of indigestion."

"Guess you won't want these, then, huh?" Tom teased, holding up the wrapped cookies still giving off aroma.

Mr. Haney tipped his hat between his thumb and index finger. "Tell your aunt thanks a million. She does do wonders substituting honey for sugar." He laid the package beside him.

Within minutes they were on their way, barreling down the highway. It was going to be a good day; Tom could feel it in his bones. He wished Willie were here. Tom turned around to study each player on the team. None held a candle to his brother. Willie had always wanted to play basketball, but couldn't for the same reason Tom never went out for band—chores. Still, Tom didn't have any regrets about helping Pa on the farm. It always made him feel like he was a part of something bigger than himself.

Willie. Sadness washed over Tom. It should be Willie on this bus on his way to play basketball. What opportunities had he stolen from his little brother? If only Tom would've had the courage then, that he had today, he wouldn't have been so selfish.

Suddenly, the bus driver slumped over the steering wheel. The bus swerved, heading directly into the path of a semi-trailer truck. Without hesitation, Tom reached over Mr. Haney's back and grabbed the wheel. Tom wrenched it as hard as he could. Within that split second, the bus narrowly avoided the oncoming disaster. Mr. Haney collapsed sideways onto Tom. The bus jerked to the right and headed for a steep embankment.

* * * * *

Lying in Walter Reed General Hospital, Willie cried. For the first time he could ever remember, he cried. Sobbed 'til his stomach and back ached. Aunt Verna's letter fell from his hand onto the shiny linoleum floor beneath his bed.

Should'a been me. Not Tommy.

Aunt Verna had written that Tommy—Tom she called him—died in an act of bravery. He had saved everyone by keeping the bus from hitting a semi-trailer truck head-on. But then the bus went over a drop-off and hit a tree, catapulting Tom through the window. He had died on impact.

Ironically, she wrote, *he had just been saved.*

Willie leaned over the bed with difficulty and retrieved the letter to reread this part. It wasn't until he read his aunt's explanation that he realized what she meant. Apparently, Tommy had had a religious conversion—"saved" Aunt Verna called it. It didn't make sense to Willie. If that was true, how could God let Tommy die?

Willie hadn't even had a chance to say goodbye. Or tell Tommy he loved him one last time.

What'll I do now? No one to live for. What purpose to go on?

Willie's gaze fell upon his bedside stand. A one-way train ticket to Cincinnati stared back at him. Aunt Verna said she would nurse him back to health. Why? So he could go on living a lie? He closed his eyes and shut out the possibilities it promised. Still, maybe it was time he allowed someone to take care of him. For once.

Maybe then he wouldn't be so scared.

"BELLY OF EARTH"

1943-45
Central Poland

What family endure is not believable. Still—I, Casimir Polasek—must tell story. News of Nazi torture and murder of Polish people explode in ears many months. We cannot believe, yet tales of horror sprout truth. 15 March 1943 nearby village Rozaniec is inferno. Eight hundred people, most women and children forced to Zwierzyniec.

During year of time for my bar mitzvah we pretend we not home. We all sad I miss most important event of my life. We live in cellar, forest, haystack. We sow crops in darkness. Papa move dirt from family graves to field and make false cover over holes in earth. Then store supplies in two tombs, prepare third for live burial for time of more German and Red Army invasion. Nazis bore into forests and villages like parasites. At last minute, we plant selves in earth. Grenades blow up in cellar few meters away. In morning, we peek from grave to see charred house.

Miracle is, horse Manya stands in field. Wagon still usable, is only blistered beside barn in ruins.

We hide in ravines, gulches. Switch often. Cover selves with sheep hides, branches and leaves. Cold is constant companion. Most friends escape to Romania. One does not. He discover our refuge and betray us.

How we survive this long is mystery. We cannot stay near farm. In blackest of night of year 1944 Papa load Grandmother, Mother, and little sister Letta into back of wagon already full of salt, withered potatoes, shriveled carrots, cured mutton, stale bread from good neighbors, jars Mother and Grandmother preserve from garden many months ago and now dug up from hidden burial, dried fruit, and jugs of water. No room for me. I protest.

Papa say, "Casimir, you must not talk." Never before I hear this harsh sound from him. "Even if no bar mitzvah, you man now and must help."

Many hours we travel rugged roads and fields. Faint light of dawn roll up darkness. We direct Manya into dense forest. Letta is hungry. Papa not allow food, only sip of water. Letta is only five years. She cry.

All day no talk aloud. Grandmother and Mother whisper under Papa's worry.

When birds roost, we set out. Again, bump through countryside. I wonder at Manya finding footing for hooves in darkest of night.

Is long trek. I walk in daze. When wagon halt, Manya stand still and stomp. Maybe to warm hooves on frozen ground. I hear men talk under breath. Someone walk in front without lantern. Papa prod Manya to follow, four kilometers, maybe five, then stop beside rocky hill of brambles and thickets.

Papa say, "Unload wagon."

Stranger make Grandmother, Mother, and Letta disappear with food bundles into rock. Papa take wagon apart. I am confused. Papa say, "Quiet. Carry boards." He load me with wood in one arm and put lighted candle in other hand.

He point at rock. Thorns prick my skin, draw blood. Briars do not want me to enter.

Inside, is cold, damp, and dark. Ahead, I see dim light of lantern, then stumble on sharp, uneven teeth of cave. I pick up boards scattered in fall. My candle flame flicker, then lose battle. I feel way to light ahead. It playing hide and seek. Shadows rise and drop. Down and round I go in narrow tunnel. I must catch footsteps and bouncing light ahead. Wood heavy in my arms.

At last I see Grandmother, Mother, Letta, and stranger. Water at feet dance in glow of lantern. Maybe pool is glad for company of humans.

By end of night we build beds and shelves from wagon. Even wheels we bring. "Can be no trace," Papa say.

"What of Manya?" I ask.

"Must not worry about Manya." Is sadness in Papa's voice.

At beginning of next day, Papa say, "We must observe *Modeh Ani*—first uttered words of day, awareness of presence of *Elohim* and thanks to Him for every breath." For many days when we wake, we are faithful.

Then, not long, maybe too long, before we not know difference of day from night, faithfulness disappear into darkness.

Grandmother tell stories; make Letta giggle. I not see Mother shake head, but know it must go side to side when she tsk with tongue at tales. Mother sing lullabies; put Letta to sleep. Papa tell secrets of childhood. Is good to know more of him. Grandmother gasp at stories she know nothing of.

When fourteen, he sneak away on prize mule of Grandfather to ride ten kilometers to see sweetheart—not Mother. Mother laugh at this. We need happy sound to warm hearts because fire not permitted for fear of smoke signaling from tunnel.

At first, we have stolen flickers of candlelight. But cave, not familiar with light, dampen matches. Lifeless candles protect secrets of cavern.

We are bears in cave for winter. Must wait for Season of Freedom. Wait. Wait. Wait. Sleep. Sleep. Sleep.

Stories from Grandmother fade into sleep. Lullabies slumber.

We feel guilt when morning prayers cease. None know when is morning. Brains not work right but we offer thanks for breath when think to do.

This is Season of Nightmare—clouds in our heads, cold, damp, hunger, cold. Drip-drip-drip off dark rock walls. Slap-slap of bat wings against chilled cave air. We do not stray far when awake. Without light, we do not see own finger to scratch nose. In darkness, we not know direction; go by hushed voice and touch. Only rouse to eat small bits of carrots or fruit with no moisture, then back to land of nothing.

Two meals each day not enough to chase away emptiness in body. Meal is maybe not right word. From small jar of beets we each take three bites. For second eating Letta and I share raw potato.

Mother pat ground where jars and sack of potatoes line cave wall. Each day she count how many left. Before we leave farm, we pack one jar of applesauce. When will come day we feast on it?

Father tie rope on rock where we sleep and stretch out to follow to spot where we relieve self. At end of rope we do duty. Soon he tie Manya's reigns to end of rope to go farther to pass body waste—must not pollute air we breathe. I cannot describe smell of belly of earth. Not musty. Can bat droppings attack nose? This smell inside earth not familiar experience.

I join Letta in pleas to exit cave. "We must endure," Papa say. "Cave is friend, protector. Eyes beyond here not friends."

"Let us escape prison for few minutes in outside dark," I beg.

Papa hush me. "We cannot trust darkness beyond walls."

Grandmother tsk-tsk. "Much evil in plan of Hitler to rid earth of Jews."

Letta say, "I hate Hitler."

Grandmother shush her. "Hatred bring more evil and darkness of soul than Hitler."

After many days—weeks?—friend of Papa bring dry matches in air-tight can. Once Mother adjust eyes, she cry at kindness, and at sight of Papa, Grandmother, Letta, and me.

I not certain of time between visits from friend of Papa who bring candles, flint, potatoes, bread, and dried-salted meat I never before taste.

Mother give thanks for Manya.

My stomach rebel. I cannot eat meat.

I must.

Thank you Manya for giving life.

We drift in—out of darkness. Eyes open, I in darkness; eyes closed, mind help me see. I think about friend in village. He not Jew. He safe. I think about what we do so bad we must hide. Papa is good man. Mother and Grandmother good womans. Letta innocent. What I do? My mind hurt trying to shovel ground of past. Cannot unearth anything worthy of exile.

I cannot stop shivering. Muscles tuck inside body to shut out cold, then shrivel, tighten.

Grandmother remind us, "Cold here not biting like snow in ravine. We survive there. We survive here."

Grandmother always right about things. Not now. She collapse in my arms and struggle with last breath. Then leave us behind.

Papa and Mother beyond sad for loss of beloved one. Also because how to bury Grandmother? Must do within twenty-four hours, Jewish custom. Mother sigh relief when friend appear same night with supplies. He reverent in removing Grandmother. He promise proper burial. Now time for *shiva*—week of mourning. Papa pray for knowledge of when seven days pass. We lose so much, cannot lose more faithfulness.

My body stiff with grief and cold. Arms and legs harden like those of Grandmother. This how life greet death?

Hunger devour me. Stomach hug backbone in grope for relief.

Is no meaning in time. Each minute same as before. Hour same as before. Day same as before. Week same as before. Month same as before. Or is minute now hour? Is month now week?

Sleep . . . only escape. Cave walls echo snores of Papa, sleep talk and nightmares from Mother. Soft, shallow breaths escape Letta. Memory of Grandmother echo in cavern. It miss Grandmother too. I cannot let her go. Eyes weep without water—none left in body. My heart pound out love for her.

One day, or night, I do not know which, Mother cannot stand. I on one side, Papa on other, we help her relieve self. She not complain; use breath left in body for humor. She say, "We people marinating in belly of earth." She force laugh, then put hand—only bones—in mine.

Papa swallow anguish—diet we all know.

Letta want me to rock her. She is rag doll in my arms. Her hair come out in clumps.

Cave drip, drip, drip. Weep for us? Or because it not like invasion of us? Result is same. Clothes damp. Blankets damp. Skin damp. Spirit damp.

I cannot endure one second more. Torture and death at hands of Nazis is welcome.

Suddenly, I wake to bright light. Whole cave shine. I warm for first time in forever.

"Wait!" I say when light fade.

Warmth stay. Sleep come in peace. I dream of sun. Freedom. Fresh air. Life beyond walls. I welcome sleep and more sleep. Land of sleep grant escape. To what? To grow old? Maybe now I in fifteenth year. I not know. How can one count time of sleep?

One day, friend of Papa come. He shout, "Nazis gone!"

Friend of Papa and other stranger carry Mother to air not damp or suffocating.

For first time in twelve months—we learn of this count— daylight flood our faces. We cannot open eyes. Sun blinding us. Time pass before eyelids cooperate. When finally they lift without clamping closed, we not recognize one another. Everyone is frail, white, withered, dirty. Only sparse, matted hair left on our heads. Eyes are dull, absent of light.

I speak and not know my voice. Before cave, my voice is high. Now, without hush whispers and echo of tunnel, my voice is deep—that of man. My body ripened without me. Yet tears make baby of me when I hear talk of millions who die.

Inside me is battle. Relief fight against shame. Joy go to war with guilt. Liberation clash with grief. Confusion, doubt flood me. Conflict drop me to my knees. I cannot utter words, but in thought give thanks for deliverance. Yet, I not understand these years. Why?

For sound mind, I must search for understanding not of own making.

I take vow to stay out of caves—to live in light, not in darkness of hatred Grandmother speak of before passing.

"BERTA'S QUESTIONS"

August, 1943
Oswiecim, Poland

As *Tante* Frieda leaned over to kiss her, Berta was surprised by warm, wet drops falling onto her cheeks. When her aunt drew her close and buried her nose in Berta's hair, she felt a tremor shoot through *Tante* Frieda's body. Until that moment, besides her aunt, the only other companion Berta had known on this journey was apprehension. Alarm now unseated it.

The long train trip from Berlin to Oswiecim, Poland had left Berta weary and wondering. *What will happen to me now?* She sighed and plopped atop the large, black trunk containing Mama's books and all of Berta's belongings—except for the gold coin tied into a handkerchief. She clutched the treasure tightly in her hand. Her legs dangled down the side of the crate, her feet barely touching the depot's platform.

"What are we waiting for?" Although she asked the question with impatience, Berta was hesitant about the next step of her travel.

"It will not be long before they approach us." Berta's aunt nodded to German soldiers strutting about the railway station.

"What is Papa like?" Berta tried not to sound scared.

Tante Frieda hugged her tighter. "At one time," she breathed into Berta's ear, "your mama loved him." She straightened, eased away from Berta.

Suddenly a soldier loomed over them. "Your papers . . . ."

Startled at the guttural barking of his voice, Berta looked up and shuddered. The curve of the soldier's lips reminded Berta of the underside of a stone arch.

Tante Frieda had their papers at the ready. "You will find everything in order."

Reading the documents with squinted eyes, the soldier studied Berta. "This states the child is eleven. She looks no more than the age of seven."

Squaring her shoulders, *Tante* Frieda replied with the air of authority Berta had come to know. "Yes, well, she doesn't take after her papa; that is for sure. This is Commandant Zeitner's daughter."

The soldier filled his chest with air. "I have no orders regarding her arrival."

"Perhaps because the Commandant is not aware of our coming." *Tante* Frieda crossed her arms, stood firm.

After an exchange of words between the two, the soldier at last commandeered a comrade in a slate-grey uniform to transport Berta and her trunk, along with her aunt, to the camp within sight of the train station.

Once in the compound, Berta found herself forgetting to breathe. With weakening knees, she followed *Tante* Frieda and two soldiers up a narrow stairwell to the second-story of what looked like a warehouse. At the top of the steps, the men led them down a long hall and into an office at the end of the corridor. The room echoed from the soldiers' boots striking the wood floor. A final thud resounded as the men dropped the trunk and pushed it against the wall beneath a window.

Berta fixed her eyes on the familiarity of the chest, a hiding place for her treasures, and for playing hide and seek. At one time, anyway. When the lid had thudded down upon her inside, she hadn't been able to push it open. Soon, she was unable to breath. Her muffled cries barely escaped the trunk. When her aunt finally discovered her, Berta was gasping for air.

Subsequently, *Tante* Frieda drilled several small holes on all four sides of the trunk and installed a spring on the lid, making it easy to open from the inside. Still, Berta shunned the trunk as a hiding place.

She tightened her fist at the memory, the coin in her palm bringing her back to the present. Berta fit her other hand snuggly into her aunt's grasp and swallowed what felt like a grape in her throat.

Suddenly, behind them, a presence filled the doorway. "Birkenau is no place for a child!" The words exploded as if discharged from a cannon.

Frightened at the bellowing, Berta burrowed into her aunt's red, wool shawl. The fabric scratched her cheeks, but it was not as rough as the man's displeasure at her sudden appearance. Daring a peek, Berta allowed one eye to study this man. *Is this my Papa?* She did not remember him as this big, this overbearing. In fact, she did not really remember him at all. Having lived with *Tante* Frieda since Mama's death, Berta had only snapshots in her mind of Papa—affixed there by Mama's stories of his efficiency, intellect, and loyalty.

Tante Frieda stiffened. "Nonetheless, Commandant Zeitner, she is your child. I am engaged to be married, and my betrothed will have none of raising another's offspring." She twisted to free Berta from her garment, yet tenderly squeezed Berta's hand still holding fast.

Why is Tante Frieda trembling? Why doesn't Papa want me? A whirlwind of other questions stormed in Berta's head.

Tante Frieda continued, "Your wife did a remarkable job of raising Berta. She is courteous and kind. You are aware from my sister's letters that she removed Berta from school when . . . things . . . got complicated in our political system. Her mission to educate Berta at home was successful. Berta is beyond her years in academics. She is articulate and well rounded, even though your wife passionately sheltered Berta from *current affairs.*"

Berta wondered why her aunt would say that, especially since her mother frequently took her to opening nights of operas, concerts, and museum's latest exhibits. The only regret Berta had was that being taught at home meant she had no contact with her friends. When Berta had asked about the why of that, Mama had said, "Certain parents poison little minds. I do not wish to have you tainted with prejudice." Was that why Mama had given away their radio?

Tante Frieda faced Papa. "I can no longer care for her."

The words, along with the catch in her aunt's voice, made Berta want to cry.

Papa puffed furiously at his cigar, filling the room with billows of foul smoke.

Berta shrank further into her only refuge. Although the shawl's coarse material offered little protection, Berta snuggled into its familiar fiber. The coin in her hand bit into her skin. Strangely, the throbbing it caused provided reassurance. The gold piece was the last thing Mama had given her. Along with instructions.

Papa roared, "Your would-be husband refuses my generous compensation?"

Tante Frieda recoiled. "You dare to call Jew plunder compensation?"

At the volley of her words, Papa's hand thumbed his holstered Luger.

With a sniff, *Tante* Frieda threw back her head. "Would you harm me in front of your daughter after her mother died of grief and a broken heart? Shoot me . . . and the secret your wife, rest my dear departed sister's soul, left with me, as to where she concealed your savings, will accompany both of us to our graves."

Papa narrowed his eyes of steel. "Have no doubt . . . when I am ready to collect my savings I will come for them."

At that, *Tante* Frieda turned on her heels and was gone. The door slammed, rattling glass panes beyond which dark smoke clouds belched skyward.

Determined not to cry, Berta climbed onto her trunk beneath the window. She crossed her legs, folded her hands in her lap. If she dared not ask a question now, then when? She fixed her gaze upon Papa's sandy hair. "What is to become of me?" Her voice sounded smaller than she meant it to.

Papa glared, but then his eyes softened. "You look like your mother." In three strides, he was across the room and beside Berta.

Enfolded in Papa's arms, she sensed his strength, his control over the situation. Pain pushed through a portal Berta had closed when Mama died. The ache generated a wave of tears that defied her tightly closed eyes and spilled onto Papa's uniform. A strange but pleasing fragrance from Papa's cheeks wafted into her nostrils. She liked this smell of him.

While still in his embrace, a light rap sounded on the door. Without waiting for an invitation, someone entered.

Berta peeked over Papa's shoulder at a beautiful woman. Not nearly so beautiful as Mama, however. The woman wore bright red lipstick and splashes of pink rouge on her high cheekbones. Her blonde hair wound on top of her head shone as if just washed.

"This is a surprise I was not expecting." The woman knit her brow.

Papa lifted Berta from the trunk and stood her on the floor. He turned to the woman. "*Fräulein* Ilse, this is Berta. My daughter."

"Of whom you have not previously spoken."

"*Mein Liebling*—my darling—I trust you will enjoy acting as governess to my child."

Ilse smiled. "Of course, *Herr* Zeitner. It will be my pleasure."

Berta noticed the smile did not reach the woman's eyes.

As Ilse neared, Berta felt a strain in the room. Not wishing to intensify the tension, Berta smiled and curtseyed. "I am very pleased to meet you, *Fräulein*."

Papa cleared his throat. "Now, I have business to attend to. You will take Berta to our quarters."

Ilse hesitated, but only briefly. "Of course, *Herr* Zeitner." She took Berta's hand and led her from the room. When the door closed behind them and they were halfway down the stairwell, Ilse let go of Berta and marched ahead. Without turning her head, she said, "You will do as I say. If I hear anything from your father of things you report to him, you will be sorry you ever intruded upon us."

Berta said nothing.

"Do I make myself clear?"

"Yes, Ilse."

"You will address me as *Fräulein*."

Berta complied but would call her Ilse in her mind.

Ilse led Berta across a corner of the compound to a wood-slatted building. Once inside, Ilse threw open a door to a very small room. "You will sleep here," she said.

"Where is my bed?" Berta asked, studying the mop, broom, and bucket in the space.

Ilse stepped into an adjacent room and returned with a blanket and pillow. She threw them on the floor. "Until your father can arrange for a bed, you will make do with these."

Berta brought the handkerchief with the coin to her cheek.

"What have we here?" Ilse reached for Berta's hand.

The outer door opened. Papa entered.

"*Herr* Zeitner, I am so glad you are here. We must get a bed for Berta. She simply cannot sleep on the floor." Ilse's voice dripped with nectar.

Papa's eyes scanned the living quarters. "We will section off that area." He pointed to the dining room.

Berta felt Ilse stiffen as she asked, "Where will we eat?"

"The kitchen," Papa said. "I'll have an officer send over a bed and cordon off Berta's room." He left.

Silence.

Then, "Do not think for one minute you have privileges here." Ilse motioned to where she had gotten the bedding. "Your father and I share that room. You are never . . . ever to go in there. Do I make myself clear?"

Berta nodded while asking herself if Papa would believe her over Ilse. Either way, Berta resolved not to stir contention for she had nowhere else to go. Sadness settled in her heart—a heart yearning for Mama.

* * * * *

She did not know when Papa had placed her in bed, but she startled awake in sorrow and darkness so severe they almost swallowed her. Mama had taught her to regard nighttime as her friend. A companion preparing her for the day ahead. *Mama.* Berta flexed her fingers, as if to touch her. Her hand was greeted with emptiness. Neither Mama nor the coin was there. Anxiety coiled around her chest. *Where is the coin?* Frantically, she swept her hand across the cool linen sheet. At last, she came upon the handkerchief under her pillow. Bringing it to her lips, she whispered, "Mama."

In the morning she arose still dressed in her clothes of yesterday. A cloak of heaviness now accompanied them. The door to Papa's bedroom was ajar. She dared peek through the slit. Snores rippled the air where Ilse lay sleeping. Papa was not there. Berta quickly put on her shoes, tied the laces, then tiptoed out of the building.

Upon entering Papa's office, she greeted him, "Good Morning, Papa."

"It promises to be," he replied.

She headed for the chest from which yesterday he had swept her up, held her close. She lifted the weighty lid and tucked the coin inside a loose piece of the trunk's lining. She would not risk losing her coin again. Satisfied it was safe, she withdrew a dress, undergarments, and socks to take back to her room. She lowered the lid and perched upon the container to peer out the window into the gray sky, determined to receive each day as it came.

In the distance, cattle cars chugged into the train station. Instead of animals, herds of men, women, and children emptied into the hands of gun-pointing soldiers.

What is happening?

As the crowd marched into her Papa's fenced-in compound, Berta reasoned the soldiers' guns were to protect the people.

But from what? And why?

Papa was at her side, rolling down the window shade. "Did you sleep well?"

"Yes, thank you." Her thoughts tumbled to the sign above the gate she had entered the day before. "Papa, what does *Arbeit Macht Frei* mean?"

"Work Sets You Free."

Berta knew what each of the words meant, yet she didn't quite understand how that worked here. "What jobs do people do in your camp?"

Papa looked at Berta. "Where is Ilse?"

Berta did not want to tell Papa of Ilse's snores. "I needed some clothes. I did not want to bother Ilse," she said, immediately sorry she hadn't called her *Fräulein.*

Papa returned to his desk. "I would like to spend time with you, but I am finalizing plans to lay railroad tracks directly from the station into our concentration camp."

"So the people won't have to walk so far?"

"Of course. To save time. By next year you will witness the ultimate in efficiency, of which only Germans are capable."

Berta could hardly wait to see the wonderment of it.

"Now, be a good girl and have Ilse fix you some breakfast."

Berta made her own breakfast that morning and every time after that when Papa wasn't there.

* * * * *

Left on her own daily, while Ilse entertained herself, Berta sat at the window of their living room, watching people pour into the yard. One day when Papa came in for lunch, Berta peppered him with questions. "Where do all the children go? So many come, but why do I have no one to play with?"

"They go with their grandmothers to the bakery." Papa laughed, setting his green uniform's medallions to dancing. He nodded toward five billowing smokestacks past the wire-fenced yards. "Bakeries."

"What stinks so? It smells awful, like the animals that burned in our barn fire."

Papa roared with amusement. "Out of the mouths of babes. Animals. Animals, indeed."

Berta did not understand how Papa could laugh at the death of any living thing.

At home when she was nine, she had heard the terror in the horses' whinnies and in the frenzied mooing of the cows, witnessed their panic, their wild dashes behind the flames. For many nights afterward, she had awakened drenched in sweat, having dreamt of futile attempts to rescue them. She had been helpless. Powerless to save even one.

One late afternoon, Berta was in Papa's office because it was warmer than her bedroom. Her governess had gone off with a man Berta hadn't seen before. Prior to her leaving, Ilse had turned off the heat.

Papa hadn't been surprised when Berta showed up. "Ilse said she'd send you over," he said. "She has shopping to do." More and more frequently, Ilse went shopping, or to her brother's, cousin's, friend's or somewhere.

Berta was thankful Papa allowed her in his office—until he had visitors. Then he swept her into the supply closet. She didn't mind because a dangling lightbulb allowed her to read and reread *Tante* Frieda's every-other-week's letters. The small space also had a blanket and shelves of books Papa had stocked it with. "Especially for you," he'd said. She could escape into a much nicer world here.

Certainly much nicer than what she witnessed as she crossed the room to the window. She raised the shade and flattened her hands against the glass barrier between her and the people below. "Papa, why do the people stand so long in the cold?" Papa did not answer. "Where are their coats? Why are they sleeping, piled in carts?" Papa had ceased answering—weeks, months ago.

As always, Papa rose from his desk and jerked down the shade. "There are some new books on the shelf for you," he said, brushing the top of her head with his lips.

Although she felt warmth from his breath, and from his heart, the possible answers to her questions created cold, dark clouds within her.

Despite his silence, from one day to the next, Berta's questions continued, sometimes in the presence of Ilse. "Why does hair spill from holes in my mattress? Why do the soldiers beat the skeleton people?"

Finally, the answers came. From Ilse. In Papa's absence, Ilse grabbed Berta by the shoulders and slammed her onto the hard kitchen chair. "Enough of your questions! Are you so daft and blind you cannot see the truth?" Ilse erupted in a tirade of stories and lies.

Berta clamped her hands over her ears. Papa could not be responsible for any of this. Mama said he had been an honorable man—one who surely could change all of this. Ilse's words tormented Berta, even in her sleep.

She made certain to never again ask questions when Ilse was within hearing. But Berta was determined to get at the truth and continued to probe her father. Finally, one especially sky-darkened day, Papa drew Berta from her trunk. "Enough questions. They have nothing to eat and are beaten because they ask questions and do not do as I say."

Papa's icy glare to beyond the window plunged fear into Berta's heart. From the corner of her eye, she caught a glimpse of a burly guard outside in the yard below wrenching a little boy from his mother. Berta's thoughts tumbled back to how she felt when death had torn her Mama away. Her gaze shifted to the sky. Ashes floated from the heavens, assaulting her nostrils despite the closed window. The odor of death enveloped her. As did Ilse's explanations. Nausea swelled within Berta.

As Papa released his grip, she backed against the chest. Only after he had returned to his desk, did Berta dare turn to lift the lid to retrieve the coin. Turned away from her Papa, she untied the handkerchief. Studying the likeness of Willhelm II on the 1901 20-Mark, she wondered what kind of a man Willhelm had been. She didn't recall studying about him. *When had terror begun? Has evil always existed?*

Through the oppressing weight of it all, her Mama's eyes came into focus, along with her lips imparting final words as she held up the gold piece. The message echoed in Berta's ears: "This is plunder . . . intended for selfish gain." Mama pressed the coin into Berta's palm. "When this madness is over, I implore you to take this coin and all of the hidden loot and use it for selfless gain." Mama coughed, gasping for air. She held Berta's gaze, then directed it to the gold Mark. Flipping it over, Mama continued, "There are two sides to every coin, my child." Her eyes pleaded with Berta. "Promise me you will add to this everything we own . . . to heal and restore those who have suffered, as much as that is possible."

Mama's entreaty, once meaningless, now made sense. The madness to which she referred had not been her death. The heaviness of the revelation pressed in upon Berta. How could she have been so blind, as Ilse had accused? Death had paraded before her eyes for months.

Papa brings about death and destruction.

She could barely breathe at the magnitude of it. She closed her eyes, wishing to shut out evil, but it descended upon her, dragging her toward a black hole and the impossibility of honoring the promise she had made to her mother.

From the abyss arose an echo of Mama's request. At first not much more than a hush, it quickly spiraled through the darkness, as if wiping soot from a blackened window. At last, Berta could see the other side of the coin. The essence of life and restoration. This was the purest possible piece Mama had entrusted to her.

I am but a child. How can I possibly redeem it?

She returned to her quarters. A note rested against a lamp. She lifted it and read, even though it was addressed to Papa. Ilse was gone. She would not return. Gladness spread through Berta. Until she looked out the window into the pain of those in the camp's barren yard. An idea sparked.

Carefully, Berta crafted her questions. She would wait for the right moment to present her petitions—when Papa would not have time to think about them or to argue her logic.

That moment arrived the morning Papa was to entertain important officers. Papa had paced back and forth, back and forth, ever since she'd entered the room. He had repeatedly looked at his watch, rearranged papers on his desk, straightened the medals on his uniform.

Quietly, Berta approached as he dropped with a grunt on the edge of a chair. "Papa, wouldn't it be best if I were not in your way?" She wrapped her arms around his neck. "What if I had a playmate?" Berta rose, walked to the window, leaned over the chest, and pointed outside to a small child herded into a line of new arrivals. "What about that one?" She turned to Papa and shrugged the innocent request.

Papa pushed back the cuff of his sleeve, checked his watch. "I suppose."

Encouraged by this progress, Berta allowed herself the unthinkable. *Two. Perhaps I can save two.* "You know I need exercise. Wouldn't the warehouse where you store goods be the perfect place to play?"

Rising, Papa tugged the front of his uniform into place. "Hmm . . . I would not have to worry about the noise you make."

Berta sighed. "But then, you might worry that I could harm myself." She skipped to Papa and pressed his hand between hers. "That girl's mother." Berta pointed to a petite woman, almost childlike in stature. "Couldn't she mind us? Oh, Papa, since I no longer have a governess, wouldn't it be better for me . . . and you . . . to have someone watch over me?"

Papa summoned his assistant. "*Herr* Schmidt, take Berta to the compound. She will select two from the masses—one who will entertain her. And a servant. Lock them in the warehouse near the firebox where it is warm. This will be Berta's daily regimen. Make certain her meals are delivered; however, her servant and the child are to receive only their usual allotment. That is all."

Berta smiled her thanks. *Dare I make one more request?*

Boot steps thundered up the stairwell.

Blood surged to her head, drummed in her ears. "Papa, can *Herr* Schmidt take my chest to the warehouse?"

Papa hesitated, then nodded *Herr* Schmidt in the direction of Berta's trunk. "Be quick about it."

Mentally measuring the container as the officer tugged it toward the door, Berta determined it to be large enough to hide the woman and child when the time was right. Berta's heart leapt, dislodging the helplessness which had too long made its home there.

"What is so heavy in here?" the officer demanded.

"Mama's books," Berta replied truthfully.

Herr Schmidt summoned another soldier to help carry the trunk.

* * * * *

The girl's name was Esther, her mother's Ruth. Much like Berta, Esther, four years younger than Berta, was small for her age. Her mother, however tiny in body, was big in courage.

Upon their first meeting in the warehouse, the Polish woman crossed her arms against her small chest, demanding in broken German, "What you want with us?"

Despite Ruth's bravado, Berta saw the trembling of the woman's jaw, the thrumming of the veins in her neck. *I have chosen well. Ruth will be cautious yet strong.* Berta smiled at her plan.

"To play with Esther while you look after us," Berta replied.

The suspicion in Ruth's eyes did not bother Berta.

"Would you like me to read to you?" Berta asked Esther.

"She no speak German," Ruth said.

"I have picture books." Berta gathered the books, sat on the floor, then patted a spot, gesturing her new playmate to join her.

Esther hesitantly looked to her mother.

Ruth nodded, then sat as well, pulling her child onto her lap.

By the end of the afternoon, Berta had gained Esther's friendship. Berta reasoned trust would not be an issue with the girl as long as her mother was present. Ruth's trust would take time. Time Berta hoped she had.

During the days afterward, haystacks of clothes provided an inviting hiding place for Esther, who burrowed into them like a rabbit. With each trainload of people, the haystacks increased in size. *Why do the people have to give them up? Do I dare plead with Papa about giving them back so they will be warm?* Already, Berta knew the answers to these questions. It was better if she didn't think about all of this.

Two weeks passed. Berta shared her meals with Ruth and Esther when the guard wasn't looking. On that first day when Berta had eaten nothing, wanting to give her servings to build her new friends' strength, Ruth had refused to eat and withheld food from Esther. Finally, Berta understood that Ruth thought Berta didn't eat because the portions were poisoned. From then on, Berta made certain to take a bite before sharing.

Still, Ruth wore suspicion like a shield. Berta did not know what she could do to gain Ruth's trust. In fact, she asked that very question. "Ruth, what must I do for you to believe I am not going to hurt you?"

Ruth squared her shoulders. "You German. I Polish Jew. How you ask question?"

This was proving to be more difficult than Berta had imagined. *Was my plan a stupid idea?*

That question loomed even larger during hide-and-seek play when Esther refused to climb into the now-empty trunk. Berta pointed out the breathing holes and the easy-to-lift lid. So, when it was Esther's turn to seek, Berta folded herself inside the container, noting as the lid shut it would be a tight fit for both Esther and Ruth, but that it was possible.

Again and again, Berta coaxed her little friend to join her in the box, to no avail. One afternoon, Esther broke out in sobs. The guard demanded to know what was going on.

That night Papa had a talk with Berta. "I've had second thoughts about you having *someone*—although I use that term loosely—to play with. The guard tells me it is not wise."

Fear snaked through Berta. Tears sprang to her eyes. Her plan was going up in smoke, just like the black clouds mushrooming from the smokestacks. "Oh, Papa, please don't take Esther away from me!"

"Esther?" A frown froze on Papa's face. "You call this . . . this Jew . . . by a name?"

At once Berta realized her mistake. "I've heard her mother call her that. She's nothing more than a distraction for me. I've read all my books. There really isn't anything else to occupy my time."

Papa chewed on his cigar. "Very well then. But if I hear further reports of problems—"

"You won't! I promise." The knot in Berta's stomach eased a bit.

The next day, Berta was careful not to upset Esther. As a peace offering—and ashamed she hadn't thought of it before— she brought a coat. *I know Papa wouldn't let this girl wear one from the piles, but surely he won't mind me giving away mine, since I've outgrown it. Mama said he was a man of efficiency. This is efficient use of what I can no longer use.* Even though it was too large for Esther, Berta hoped it would stop the girl's shivers that accompanied her each morning to the warehouse. "This is for you." Berta held out the coat.

Ruth swept it aside. "Others . . . already believe I your spy."

Berta reeled back. *What grief have I brought to Ruth and her daughter?* Shame and regret welled within her. *How can I make it up to them?*

When Berta's twelfth birthday arrived, she convinced Papa's cook to bake her a small cake. She would save a piece for him, even though he hadn't mentioned her special day. Berta concealed the cake inside a small box on the way to the warehouse. By the time she arrived, the frosting was smeared, but otherwise the cake was intact. She selected a shawl from the haystack of clothes and spread it out on the floor for a picnic.

She summoned Ruth and Esther. The little girl clapped her hands and skipped hurriedly to the spot offering a treat.

"It is my birthday today," Berta said.

Tears breached the rim of Ruth's eyes.

"What is wrong?" Berta asked.

"Esther turn eight three days back."

Berta's heart swelled. "Then this is her birthday cake."

They all quickly devoured the entire cake before the guard made his rounds.

Papa would have to wait until next year for a piece.

* * * * *

That night, lost in sadness, Berta drifted in and out of sleep. *Whatever can I do to help my dear friends?*

Out of one of these chasms her mother's voice arose from a time long ago. "You mustn't despair, for it will rob you of your purpose." The sweet sound evaporated.

Berta sat up, opened her eyes, willing her mother's face to appear. She waited and waited. Finally, dawn edged out the blackness, bringing with it Berta's determination and hope.

At a breakfast of black bread and much coveted berry jam, Papa slapped a letter on the table. "Frieda has lost her husband. Seems he was conscripted then sent to the front lines." Papa puffed on his cigar.

Berta still hadn't gotten used to the foul smell.

"Your aunt wants to take you back." He glanced at Berta.

She dared not smile, even though the news rushed like a warm bath through her.

"Pity. You and I have just gotten to know one another." He rose. "You are to leave in an hour."

"Is she coming for me?"

"How could she? I just this morning received the letter."

"Are you going on the train with me?"

"No. You are twelve now. A young lady. I meant to celebrate with you but I have important matters on my mind." Papa reached into his desk drawer and pulled out an envelope. "You and your aunt can shop for whatever you want for your present," he said.

Papa handed her the envelope, then began pacing. "Besides, I cannot leave the camp. One of our *Führer's* Generals is expected to arrive this afternoon to inspect the compound."

"An hour is too soon for me to be ready!" The warmth inside Berta turned to ice. She scraped her chair back. "I'll have to pack."

"No need. I'm certain Frieda will want to outfit you anew, since you've grown some."

Berta's mind scrambled for reason. "I would at least like to take my trunk. It means so much to me. As well as Mama's books . . . and the ones you gave me," she hurried to add. "They are all in the warehouse. I'll hurry." She scurried away to avoid argument.

On the way, she hoped Ruth and Esther would already be there. *What if they're not there? Even if they are, how will I ever get Esther to get into the trunk?*

Everything seemed impossible.

"You mustn't despair, for it will rob you of your purpose," her mother's encouragement repeated in her head.

Berta tried not to run, for fear of alerting the guards' suspicion. Arriving at the warehouse, she slowly opened the door, hoping beyond hope. There beside her trunk sat the two she had come to love.

Hurrying to their side, Berta lowered her voice. "Where is the guard?"

"He deliver us. Say he be right back," Ruth said.

Berta quickly explained the situation and her plan.

Ruth shook her head. "We be found out. Killed."

Anxiety rushed at Berta. "What have you got to lose? You know what has happened to the people who came the same time you did." She hated to fling such a horrid fact in Ruth's face, but it was time for drastic measures. "Hurry. We don't have a second to lose."

The doorknob rattled. The door squeaked partially open. Someone spoke to the guard at the door. He let the heavy wooden panel slam shut.

Fear flashed across Ruth's face. She spoke lovingly, yet sternly to her child. Ruth climbed into the trunk and held out her arms to her daughter. Esther balked. Ruth coaxed. Berta gently lifted Esther up and cradled her in her mother's arms.

The door opened.

Berta closed the trunk lid and locked it. She pocketed the key.

"I'm ready," she said to the guard. "Papa will have you haul my trunk to the train."

The guard shouted to another guard, summoning him to help. They grunted as they lifted the container. "Why is this so heavy?" one demanded, looking around.

"My books are precious to me," Berta said in truth.

"Where are the Jews?" They let the trunk thud to the floor.

"They couldn't stay with me leaving, as I'm sure you are aware." Berta nodded to the door. "Papa said to hurry. The train leaves soon."

The guard attempted to lift the trunk lid. "Why won't this open?"

"It gets stuck in cold weather. It's not warm enough in here yet to unswell it." Berta marched toward the door, then turned to glare at the soldiers. "Papa won't be happy if I miss the train."

* * * * *

At the station, Berta insisted on them depositing her trunk in her private sleeping car. Not until the train had chugged several miles down the track did she dare slip her key into the lock. She lifted the lid expecting to see terror in Esther's eyes. Instead, she slept peacefully, snuggled tightly against her mother.

"It's alright to get out. You are safe. Although if there is a rap at the door, you'll have to slip quickly back into the box," Berta said. "We have a toilet here, and Papa ordered meals delivered to my compartment. I expect to arrive at my aunt's house in a few days."

Berta decided to spend the trip teaching Esther to speak German. The child was a quick learner. While they still couldn't carry on a conversation, Berta contented herself with watching Esther revel in her accomplishments. At times, the little girl got so excited she shrilled with delight. Berta worried they would be overheard.

The second day of the journey, a rap sounded on the door.

Terror crossed Ruth's face. She scooped Esther into her arms and hurriedly nestled them both into the trunk.

Berta opened the door, just a little.

A woman stood in the corridor. "I saw you arrive alone and thought you might welcome some company," she said. "My name is Judith."

Berta hesitated, her mind scrambling for a response.

"Of course, if you prefer to be alone—"

"Would you like me to come to your cabin?" Berta asked.

"Yes, of course. I'll have tea and biscuits sent." The woman gestured to her adjacent compartment.

Once settled, Berta commented that Judith's accent led her to believe she was a foreigner.

"I am from America," she said.

Berta thought Judith must be very brave to leave a land of safety to enter such dangerous territory. Or perhaps she was a spy. Berta was careful during the next hour to guard her words. She shared nothing of losing her mother or having left her father's concentration camp. She only stated that she was traveling to her aunt's.

The following afternoon, Judith once again presented herself at Berta's door with another invitation. Again, Berta suggested they go to Judith's cabin.

Sipping her tea, Judith raised her eyes, obviously studying Berta.

Berta squirmed in her seat.

"I know you are alone in your room, but I keep imagining the voice of a child." Judith cradled her cup in the saucer.

Berta froze.

Judith smiled. "I am not the enemy."

Berta forced a smile and excused herself.

* * * * *

The train whistle shrilled, announcing Berta's arrival home. Her heart hammered in her chest. *Tante* Frieda knew nothing of the surprise awaiting her. Berta wasn't exactly certain of her aunt's political sympathies, but she hoped they aligned with her sister's—Berta's mother.

The train rolled to a stop. Berta spied her aunt on the platform, her eyes anxiously searching the compartment windows. Three guards paced by her side. Berta knew immediately what they were waiting for. She stepped into the hallway. Judith walked toward her. *It's now or never.*

Berta lowered her voice. "I'm in need of help."

Judith's eyebrows raised.

"I left my father's house taking things I knew my aunt would want—without his permission. He has sent soldiers to retrieve my trunk." Berta started to cry. "Papa simply can't have them back. My mother is dead and it's all that's left for my aunt. And for me."

"How can I help, dear?"

"I noticed a trunk in your cabin."

Judith nodded.

"Would you mind changing rooms with me, so when the soldiers board they can check your trunk and see that what Papa thinks I took, they'll see he was mistaken?"

"I guess there is no harm in that." She handed Berta her trunk key.

"As soon as they leave, I'll retrieve my trunk, and no harm is done."

Judith smiled conspiratorially. "You, my dear child, are going to make something of yourself in this world."

"You sound like my mother," Berta replied, stepping to enter Judith's cabin just as the armed men bolted down the passageway, her aunt on their heels. Berta opened the door and turned to greet them. "*Tante* Frieda!" she cried, spreading her arms.

The soldiers shoved her aside and entered "her" compartment. They went straight to the trunk and tried to pry it open. "Where is the key?" Steel-blue eyes bored into Berta.

She thrust a hand in her pocket. Her fingers touched two keys, electrifying her with terror. What if she gave them the wrong one?

"*Beeile dich!*" The command for her to hurry zinged through her.

Berta fumbled with the keys, hoping she would pick the right one. As her hand pulled from her pocket, the soldier grabbed her arm and wrested the key away.

He forced it into the lock.

Berta held her breath.

Click.

She exhaled. "What is this all about?" she dared ask. *Tante* Frieda's comforting hands rested on her shoulders.

The trunk lid flew open, revealing clothes and shoes. The soldiers rifled through the contents, throwing everything out. "Where did you get these?"

Steeling herself, words flew out of Berta's mouth. "I . . . I confess I took things from the warehouse. There were so many things. I just wanted to bring something to my aunt." She tilted her head back to look up at *Tante* Frieda.

Her aunt's mouth dropped open, her eyes widened. Her grip on Berta's shoulders tightened.

"Where are they?" A soldier demanded, shoving Berta against the doorframe.

Berta staggered, then caught her balance. She pointed at the clothes strewn about the room. "That is everything." She stared back at the man whose hand had gone to the gun in his holster.

"Don't play ignorant," he growled. "Where are those filthy Jews?"

Tante Frieda stepped fully into the room. She gathered the clothes and shoes and packed them into the trunk.

"Answer me!" the soldier ordered.

"I don't know what you are talking about."

"That woman and child from the warehouse."

"Oh, them. I expect they returned to their bunks."

Finished putting everything back into the trunk, *Tante* Frieda straightened. "Now that you have seen the child has nothing of value to hide, would you load this into my motorcar? I'll be sure to report to Commandant Zeitner of your courtesy in helping his *innocent* daughter."

When the men at last managed the trunk out and onto the station's platform, they easily carried it to *Tante* Frieda's Zeppelin.

"You will need to fold back the canvas top as the vehicle's trunk won't accommodate Berta's box," *Tante* Frieda instructed. "Be careful to spread those on the seat to prevent damage." She pointed to patchwork quilts piled in the back.

While the men loaded her trunk, Berta searched the train window for Judith. As the train huffed away, she spied her. As they locked eyes, Berta then remembered the key in her pocket. *Did I lock Ruth and Esther inside?* Berta's throat constricted. Judith would not be able to get them out. At least not without involving someone else. Someone who would likely betray them.

The soldiers stood on the platform, their gaze roaming the area.

When her aunt drove away, Berta was at least relieved that Judith had not gotten off here because soldiers were stopping those with trunks and demanding them opened.

Tears streamed down Berta's face for the duration of the five-kilometer-ride home. Upon arrival at the cottage, she dried her eyes, afraid her aunt would think she was unhappy about returning.

Tante Frieda scooped Berta into her arms. "I would have come to Poland for you, but I was waiting for your father's permission."

"It . . . it is not that," Berta stammered.

"There. There. It's alright, dear. You are safe now. Those awful men are gone."

Berta burst into tears. Between sobs, she spilled the whole story.

Her aunt listened patiently, all the while stroking Berta's hair.

"Without the key, they can't get out. I've killed Ruth and Esther."

"Now, now. Have you considered another possibility? Might you have closed the lid and forgot to lock the trunk?"

Berta's sobs stuttered to a stop. She felt a rush of hope. *But what will happen to my friends?*

Three days later, Papa stormed into the house. "Where are they?"

The fury in his voice and face frightened Berta. "Wh . . . who?" she asked, her words shaky.

"The prisoners I *trusted* you with." Without waiting for a response, he turned and motioned for a small troop to ransack the house, searching for false walls, loose floorboards, and any place that might conceal the Jews.

At the end of the afternoon of probing to no avail, Berta approached her father. "Papa, as you can see, they are not here. Nor do I know where they are. I promise you that."

Papa snorted something about the cost of losing prisoners and left as abruptly as he'd come.

* * * * *

Over the next few months, Berta settled into routine. It felt good to return to normalcy and love. Yet, thoughts of Ruth and Esther kept Berta from being at peace.

Until the day she received a letter from America.

> Dear Berta,
>
> I learned of your full name from our mutual friends. As a journalist, I have access to sources that assist me in ferreting out ways to reach people.
>
> Please know I am well and have had the wonderful opportunity to complete the assignment. Do not concern yourself with my things. They mean nothing compared to the wonderful experience you shared with me.
>
> That is all for now, except you will notice I did not include my return address. I am sorry you will not be able to contact me.
> Your American Friend, Judith

Berta smiled at the peace in her heart that Judith's message brought. She reached for Mama's coin on the desk beside her.

"Mama," she murmured, pressing the coin to her heart. "Ruth and Esther are safe because of you and the encouragement you gave me. Now I know I can make a difference and eagerly await my next opportunity."

Her aunt's words in Papa's office about Mama's buried treasures sprang to Berta's mind.

An idea sprouted.

"INTERNMENT CAMP"

May 23, 1944
Crystal City Internment Camp, Texas

I am fifteen years old and a prisoner.

My birth name is Kaori Kajioka. I prefer to be called Kay. I am in Crystal City Internment Camp, Texas, tenth grade class. My assignment is to keep this diary. Mrs. Murakami said we can write whatever we want and no one else will read it. She said it will be good for me because I am shy about expressing myself out loud.

Except to my bosom friend Shirley at home in Everett, Washington. Even then, I do not write my true thoughts to her, as all mail is censored, or so the rumor goes. I want to share my innermost feelings with Shirley, but I am not certain what they are. Everything inside me is jumbled and doesn't make sense.

I miss Shirley terribly. She promised to store my most prized possessions—a photograph of my grandparents, the heart necklace Shirley gave me on my last birthday, and a jewelry box my grandfather made for me. I cross my fingers that she can get into our house, and that things are as we left them.

Government officials came to take Father away in what they called "evacuation efforts." Later, we joined him in this camp. In the rush and confusion to be transported, we had only a short time to take what we could carry in our suitcase. I feel guilty for not packing the items I asked Shirley to retrieve. Our house was in a frenzy. Who could think clearly?

I have never seen so many Japanese in my life. At home, I was the only Japanese in my class. Yet, I felt more of a belonging there than here. I do not speak Japanese and have no desire to do so. I am an American. To be pro-American here in camp is unpopular. It is more acceptable to be Buddhist than Christian. I keep my convictions to myself and do not wish to trade my faith for acceptance.

* * * * *

June 2, 1944

I used to like to go camping, but I hate it here. A ten-feet high cyclone fence topped with barbed wire surrounds us. Cockroaches scamper under the wood buildings where black widow spiders also lurk. Huge red ants are everywhere. A rattlesnake bit Etsuko last week. This is not my idea of camping. Still, I must not be handicapped by hatred. I have other barriers to surmount that are not of my making.

Father, Mother, and I are housed in a duplex. We have our own kitchen with an oil stove and refrigerator. We share a bathroom with a family of six on the other side. Although there is a central facility in camp for washing bedding, we launder our clothing in tubs in our own room.

Mother goes to the canteen once weekly to get our food supply. Although we do not go hungry, my mouth waters at the memory of her Pacific Ocean baked salmon.

* * * * *

July 9, 1944

The pencil slips in my grip as I attempt to write. The heat and humidity are unbearable.

* * * * *

October 2, 1944

I have not been faithful in my writing. I have been busy studying mathematics and science. Today, in biology class we dissected an ugly horned toad. Itsuri tried to taunt me with it. I refused to play along, which only incited him to throw a doodle bug in my face. Good advice from the Bible to turn the other cheek. The bug ricocheted off my skin and went down the front of his shirt. Itsuri proved he will not have to take the jitterbug classes they offer here one night every week.

* * * * *

December 1, 1944

Today I celebrate my sixteenth birthday. Perhaps celebrate is too strong a word, even though Father and Mother plan a party for me this evening. If I were home, I would invite Shirley. I wonder if she is thinking of me and my special day. Her life is going on without me there. I suspect she doesn't tell me everything she is doing because she doesn't want me to feel excluded. If only her withholding could protect me from feeling left out.

* * * * *

December 8, 1944

I received a card from Shirley today. The postmark shows she mailed it in plenty of time for me to have gotten it on my birthday. I am so glad she remembered. She said Andy Wilson said to tell me hi and happy birthday.

Andy was going to ask me out on a date when I turned sixteen. I was nervous about Father letting me go since Andy is a year older than I am. More and more, he appears in my dreams. Last night he kissed me.

* * * * *

January 8, 1945

Shirley wrote that she is not dating anyone. She is so pretty I cannot imagine boys not asking her out.

There are many boys here my age—not only Japanese but German and Italian. Some of them are quite handsome. Mother smiles when Itsuri comes around. She thinks he is sweet on me. Sweet is not a word I use to describe him.

I will wait for Andy.

* * * * *

July 4, 1945

Independence Day. For whom?

* * * * *

July 15, 1945

I joined the Little Theater and have discovered another avenue of expressing myself. There I find courage to be what I otherwise cannot. My shyness is shelved for a period in time while I experience freedom in a body foreign to me. Whereas books afford me the luxury of internal escape, theater allows that and an outward soaring as well.

The Bible tells me things will work together for good because I love the Lord and He chose me for His purpose. So, had I not been imprisoned here, I fear I would have never known the joy and exhilaration of acting. I have discovered a new part of me—one which has permission to spring to life. I am a prisoner, yet I am not.

Is it possible professional acting is in my future? Hope allows me to envision a life beyond these fences.

* * * * *

July 25, 1945

School is not in session, so I ordered some books from the local library. They came today, and I am excited to lose myself in their pages. At least I can go away for a while and escape the blistering sun that bakes our roofs. Although my skin responds to the sweltering, my mind draws in the cool of Jack London's snow.

Camp officials encourage us to attend movies they offer. I suppose this is one way to keep our minds from straying elsewhere.

* * * * *

August 1, 1945

The kibeis are talking of returning to Japan after the war. Perhaps it is best if they do. The kibeis are American born, like me, but they went to school in Japan. Their faces display their resentment and bitterness over prejudice. With too much time on their hands, they spend hours talking and fanning the flames of hatred. I am glad I do not understand all of what they say since they combine Japanese with English language.

My time is better spent working. I earn ten cents per hour helping in the food distribution center. News reports state there is a shortage of farm labor especially in the midwest, therefore crops are rotting in the fields and those of us in internment camps should be thankful we receive whatever allotments the government can spare. It seems to me the government could have saved itself a lot of trouble by not imprisoning us here in the first place. Then they wouldn't have to feed us.

* * * * *

August 14, 1945

Japan surrendered today! Shouts of joy fill the air. In all my life I have never seen people so gay. For some, jubilation is not because Japan surrendered but because our release is imminent. Father warns it is too soon to know what is ahead. He fears it may be a dragon waiting to pounce on us. Mother attempts to hush his warnings but the possibilities have already sprouted wings. As for me, I can hardly bear my anticipation of seeing Shirley.

* * * * *

September 29, 1945

Release has not yet visited some of us in camp. This has been my residence for too many months. I cannot fathom this incarceration stretching further. I am anxious to go home. There is talk of what awaits us. Will Father be able to return to Boeing where he was an Engineer? Will our house be intact? Will my classmates look at me the same as before? Perhaps I will be an eyesore, a reminder of their brothers or fathers killed or tortured in the War. Will I be able to walk down sidewalks and greet neighbors without shame—a mantle that is not mine to wear? Will my innocence have any merit?

My friend Shirley assures me through her letters that nothing has changed between us. How can that be true? I am not the same as before. When we were arrested, my body and mind were those of a child. Both have expanded.

Is Shirley the same person I left behind? Will she feel guilt over having not shared everything with me? If she cannot lock eyes with me I will know things are not the same.

* * * * *

February 13, 1946

I cannot contain myself. Nor do I wish to. I have had enough containment for one lifetime. Today, I refuse to let apprehension leap on me. I will not allow anger to imprison me. Nor will I be captive within walls of unforgiveness.

Tomorrow, I will shield myself from fear's talons with faith—faith and trust that *all* things work together for good.

When the sun rises, I will walk through the barbed arms and not look back.

I pray Shirley's eyes welcome me home.

"PLAYING WAR"

1944
Normandy Coast of France

Ever since the June 6th invasion, twelve-year-old Henri Gustard could neither think nor talk of anything else. The Americans had come. Even though the war still raged in Europe, the Germans no longer terrorized his village.

On that spring morning, Henri had risen early in the attic bedroom of his family's country cottage. Peering out the garret window, he could barely contain his excitement as the lifting fog revealed a sea of small boats landing on Normandy's beaches. Glancing down the country lane, he witnessed the chaos of Nazi soldiers running away from the beach.

Now late summer, Henri's excitement turned toward today's promise of adventure. His cousin Émile, age ten, would arrive shortly from Paris for a visit before returning to classes. Living in a houseful of girls, Henri welcomed the prospect of a boy with whom he could play war. Henri's older sisters, Florette and Gabrielle, and younger ones Simone and Colette did not appreciate the finer elements of strategy or falling down dead.

His friends Albert and Claude had not yet returned from Holidays, and Henri was bored with his daily chores of milking the cow, cleaning the horse stall, and piling scythed field grass into haystacks. Why couldn't he have Simone's fun job of gathering eggs? That was like finding buried treasure—even if the old hen Henrietta did draw blood with piercing pecks.

Henri jumped into his trousers and slipped suspenders over his tanned shoulders. He attacked the narrow, winding attic steps two at a time, breezing down the stairwell, through the kitchen and out to the barn.

"*Bonjour*, Nellie." He patted the cow on the rump. As he set about washing her teats, he thought about the American Joe who had named her Nellie. At the first sound of it, Henri had adored the way it rolled off his tongue. "Nellie. Nellie." American Joe lingered in Henri's thoughts. The man with the bushy eyebrows had come to their farm after having gotten separated from his troop. Although he'd only stayed a day, the man had ingrained himself into Henri's mind as a hero.

Nellie mooed. Henri set about his task, his fingers agile and his hands strong from three years of milking. He finished two teats quickly and moved without missing a stroke to the next. When almost done, he twisted his wrist, aimed for his face, and squeezed. Frothy, white milk filled his mouth. He licked his lips then swiped them with the back of his hand.

An automobile purred into the barnyard. Henri heard chickens cackle; the flapping of their wings filled the air. Emerging from the barn, Henri set down his full pail and ran to greet Émile.

Émile's mother intercepted Henri with a hug. "My how you've grown in just a year's time." She kissed him on both cheeks before turning to her own son. "Émile, be a dear and bring the bags into the house."

Dragging the luggage through the parlor door, Henri overheard his mother and aunt in the kitchen talking about the war and how his aunt had braved the roads to visit their farm. Before the war, his aunt and uncle had driven up from Paris at least once a month. Now, it was because of the *gazogene* affixed to the side of the motorcar that she was able to make this trip. Henri had heard of this contraption but had not seen one before today. Since gasoline was unavailable, the *gazogene*—a coal-burning device—was the only way they could motor about.

His mother and aunt's voices hushed. Henri caught snatches of the conversation. "French underground . . . missing . . . frightened." Henri had suspected his uncle was part of the French underground movement from bits and pieces he had made out from eavesdropping on his parents. He wondered if his uncle had gone missing, and if this were the reason his aunt dared travel alone with Émile. Maybe they would stay a long while.

The women's voices returned to normal. "My mouth has watered all morning in anticipation of fresh cream to stir into a brew from these last bits of coffee grounds I saved for this occasion," his aunt said.

Henri scurried out the door to retrieve his bucket of milk with its cream at the top. Outside, he skidded to a halt. His dog had beaten him to it. He shooed the canine away just as his sister Florette rounded the corner of the house. Henri ignored her suspicious glance.

After a breakfast of camembert cheese spread on freshly baked bread and blueberries that Gabrielle had picked yesterday, Émile helped Henri finish his chores.

Simone and Colette appeared. "You are to watch us," five-year-old Simone announced, her hands on her hips. Three-year-old Colette nodded her head and picked her nose.

Henri groaned. "Watch you do what?"

"Wherever you go, we get to go, too." Barefoot, Simone drew a circle in the dirt with her big toe.

"We're going to war. Girls can't. You'll just get hurt. Besides, why can't Florette or Gabrielle mind you?"

"They're helping in the kitchen," Simone said. Colette enthusiastically nodded her head, sending her dark curls to bounce around her ears.

"Too bad." Henri huffed off to the tool shed where he kept a rifle he had carved from a tree limb.

"I'm telling." Simone raced to the house.

In the shed, Henri gathered his armor—a canvas knapsack filled with rocks for grenades, his rifle, a thin board with a whittled point for a sword, and a butter knife for a dagger.

"HENRI!"

Henri's shoulders dropped, along with his hope for adventure.

"Henri, you are to be in care of your little sisters today. Do NOT go past the fence at the edge of the trees and do NOT lose sight of them." Henri's mother's word was final.

"Simone and Colette can be the enemy," Émile said. He grabbed hold of Henri's arm. "I have only read in the newspaper about the invasion at the beaches. Can you take me there?"

"We are not allowed on the beach. There are still land mines."

"Father told me about them—the silent soldiers he calls them. He said it takes seven kilograms of pressure to activate them. Let's find rocks weighing that, then toss them ahead of us like grenades."

Henri shook his head. "I don't know if we can throw a seven-kilogram rock very far."

Émile pumped his muscles. "Sure we can. What are you, a coward?"

A coward Henri was not. He allowed his imagination to discharge. *We will be heroes if we rid the beach of danger.*

If Simone and Colette stayed far enough behind them, they would be safe. Besides, Colette was tiny and probably didn't even weigh seven kilograms.

Rummaging in the shed, Henri found a burlap sack and handed it to Émile. "Put your rocks in here." He strapped on his knapsack, grabbed his rifle and marched out the door. "Girls, fall in behind." He turned to salute them.

Simone and Colette high-stepped in line as they had all seen the German soldiers do.

On the way to the beach, Émile told of the frequent air raids he had experienced in Paris. Henri, absorbed in the telling, suddenly remembered his sisters. He turned to raise a hand to shield his eyes from the sun and spotted two tiny figures in the distance. "We'll wait for the girls," he said, pulling Émile to the grass beside the dirt path. Minutes later, Simone and Colette straggled near enough for Henri to hear Colette complaining that her legs couldn't walk any more. Henri sighed, walked back to hoist her to his chest and carried her the rest of the way. This would build his muscles for lobbing heavy rocks onto mines.

As they marched on, a sand dune came into view. Quickly setting Colette down, Henri dropped to his belly, legs out behind. "Enemy ahead!"

Colette started to cry.

"Shush. You'll alert the Germans of our location." Henri clapped a hand over her mouth.

Simone grabbed her little sister and sank to the ground. "Don't scare her." She scooped Colette onto her lap.

Émile, now face down, crawled toward the beach, dragging the heavy sack of grenades behind.

Henri warned the girls, "Stay here and stay down." He joined his cousin in the sneak attack. "I see something sticking out of the ground to your right." Henri motioned to a stick protruding from the sand.

"Right you are." Émile rolled a rock from the bag, stood, then raised the stone above his head. "Take cover," he shouted. The small boulder arched into the air and thudded to the ground two meters away.

Henri held his breath. American Joe had told him the fuse would delay firing until the count of four after the mine was triggered. American Joe had taught him to count, "One thousand one. One thousand two. One thousand three. One thousand four." Silence. Henri's heart thrummed against his chest. His mouth felt as dry as the dust in his fist. Finally, he exhaled. The rush of adrenaline spurred him on. He gestured straight ahead. Five meters, he mouthed, flashing five fingers.

Émile nodded. Together they inched forward. "I see it," he whispered. When within tossing distance, Émile rolled another stone from the bag. This time Henri picked it. Rising to his full height and then some on his toes, he sent the rock airborne. "Take cover!" He dropped to the sand. "One thousand one. One thousand two. One thousand three. One thousand four." Silence. Henri could hardly contain the thrill of battle. His eyes scanned the terrain. There, some twelve meters to the right, he saw it. A steel rod emerged from the sand. He signaled his cousin. Émile raised a thumb.

Without warning, Colette came running from that direction. Henri's insides turned to granite. But only momentarily. Springing to his feet, he shouted, "STOP!"

Colette held a seashell in the air. "Henri, Henri, see, see!" Her chubby feet sprayed sand in her wake.

Henri's mouth went dry, but still he forced another warning for his tiny sister to stop. Why did she never obey him? She continued to scamper toward him. As if in slow motion, he watched as she tried to jump over the rod. When she came down on top of it, Henri stopped breathing. Then, the click sent chills through Henri's body and sent him flying through the air to get to Colette. His foot caught in seaweed, slamming him to the sand. He clawed the ground for a grip to get up and get going. He must reach his sister before—

One thousand four.

The deafening explosion was followed by an echo and the still silence of Colette's mangled figure. An unbearable roar rose within him and ricocheted throughout his body, triggering an echo that would never be silenced. At that moment, Henri knew he would forever be at war.

"daddys little valentine"

February 14, 1945
Detroit, Michigan

i peekded out the window and seed daddys army friends get out of a green car

YAY YAY

i knowed daddy would remember i knowed it cause at christmas when daddy leaved he told me pauline I will send you something special on the day you turn three

thats today

the men stompded snow off their boots on the porch before they comed in the house

mommy telled me to go upstairs

i runned up to my room to get the heart i cutted out of red paper for daddy and when i comed back down i heared the man tell mommy he didnt suf fer

mommy handed johnny to the army man

he holded our baby in the air

the other man putted his fingers sideways over one eye and salooted just like daddy when he telled me i was his little soldier and to be good til he seed me again

one of the soldiers stickded something on johnnys jammies

i comed closer and seed it was a purple ribbon with a
heart

hey thats my present i telled daddys friend

he acted like he had something in his throat

mommys eyes wetted up she telled me yes your right
pauline this is something very special from daddy she taked it
off johnny and gived it to me

i gived my red paper heart to daddys friend and telled
him to make sure my daddy gets this

the army man wipeded his eyes and leaved

i runned to my room and drawed a special picture for
daddy

for when he comes home

"GOING PLACES"

April, 1945
Fort Collins, Colorado

In her sixteen years, Addie Stein had learned proper timing for treading softly. Today required such cautious steps around her mother.

"I don't care how hard up we are, Oliver. I *will not* have a German set foot on this property!" Bertha Stein slammed the lid onto a pot of boiling potatoes. "We are being invaded . . . right here in Fort Collins. Of all places, you'd think Colorado would be far enough away from Krauts and Nips."

Addie spooned flour into a cup and added cream, stirred. When 1945 began, she had hoped for better things, but in March a balloon carrying incendiary devices had landed and exploded on a nearby farm. It liked to have scared the peewaddens out of all Larimer County. They'd learned the Japanese had launched at least 9,000 such balloons the previous November, hoping to create fires and chip away American morale. All it had served to do was ignite the anger of U.S. citizens.

Mother fumed. But not just about that. This morning after a breakfast of bacon and eggs, Addie's father had announced he would take advantage of the nearly 700 German POWs being brought in to help with sugar beet crops needing to be thinned.

"Prisoners'll be here April fifteenth," he said, then walked out the door.

Addie knew that in the week between then and now, there would be no peace in the house.

Even though her mother had put in her two cents' worth, Addie knew it didn't amount to much. She smiled at the pun but just as quickly frowned at the result. Women around these parts had never had any say. *That's not exactly true*, she thought. Last September, the people of Colorado adopted a constitutional amendment providing for women to serve on juries. Even if she wasn't old enough to vote, the prospect of someday having a voice on a jury excited her.

"Soon as our men are home from war, women won't need to fill in. Things'll get back to the way they should be," Addie's father had said.

Addie hoped he was wrong. She yearned for change. Although never having been more than twenty-five miles from the farm, one day, she knew, she would dare to venture out, go places—perhaps even cross the State Line.

The gravy bubbled. Addie picked up a potholder and scooted the skillet off the firebox chamber onto the stove's side-shelf, and absently wiped her hands on her apron.

Seated, Father waited to be served. Addie was struck by a sudden awareness of the stark contrast of his rough, sun-baked hands against the smooth, baked-white enamel of the kitchen tabletop. At once, she felt sorry for him. He worked hard to provide for her and her mother. If only he weren't so pig-headed. But maybe that's what helped him endure drought, hail storms, tornadoes, grasshoppers, and an angry wife. Addie tried hard to win his approval—even if he never noticed.

"Jerrys dirty their hands killing Jews, they can danged well put their filthy mitts to good use on a Jew's farm. Way I look at it." Father grabbed a fork in one hand, a knife in the other, signaling the end of discussion. Addie's mother clamped her mouth into a flat line. Father had spoken. Any more from Mother would only incite him further.

* * * * *

Straining under the weight, Addie carried two buckets of water to the field. Carefully setting the pails down, she dipped from one and filled a tin cup. She offered it to a German soldier.

As he stood and straightened from thinning beet plants, sweat poured off his forehead. *"Danke schön."* His eyes—searching sky-blue eyes—met hers.

Instantly, she scanned the field for her father. Her stomach relaxed when she saw him scrutinizing rows with his back to her. She knew her father was too busy counting heads, still nervous because this morning's truck had simply rolled up and dumped off twenty-one Nazis. The driver said they couldn't spare a guard but assured Father POWs were carefully screened on the East Coast before being sent West. Big-time Nazis had already been weeded out.

"These prisoners won't be a problem. They're relieved to be alive and are glad to be working in fresh air as opposed to being locked up," the driver had said.

Nonetheless, Addie remembered her parents' admonition not to talk to the enemy. She did not look again at the soldier's face but snatched the cup from his hand and moved quickly to the next man bent down pulling up roots. She could feel a gaze fixed upon her. Eyes of a man who had killed. Killed her father's people in Europe.

"You're a Jew," Father had said on more than one occasion. "Never forget your heritage."

"You are French." Her mother's constant reminding rang in her head. *"You have royal blood in your veins."*

From what Addie had learned in World History, having a French king in her lineage wasn't something to brag about. Although she did like her dark eyes with long, black eyelashes. They helped her feel feminine in the midst of the man's work she was often expected to do—when she wasn't working in the kitchen.

All Addie knew for certain was that she was a farmer's daughter. And if her father had his way, she would become a farmer's wife. Father had his eye on his friend's son. Benjamin Rosen was eighteen and one of the hardest workers this side of the Rockies. Addie's mother liked the prospects because Mrs. Rosen was also French. *"At least this will keep your bloodlines as pure as they can be at this point."* Mother's words had a way of staying put in Addie's head.

Rebellion simmered in her veins. She laughed at the image of her blood boiling. On second thought, maybe it was the unusually hot May day that burned through her skin. Whichever, she knew she had this summer plus next year—her senior year of high school—to make sense of her life. How could she please Father, appease Mother, and do what *she* wanted? *I don't have to figure it out right now*, she reasoned, her back and arms aching from yet another trip from the well to the field with heavy buckets of water. Shielding her eyes from the sun, she studied its position in the sky. She must hurry back to start the noon dinner, which meant another trip to the coal bin.

Once inside the shed, she shoveled coal into a scuttle before hauling it, banging against her leg, to the kitchen. At the stove, she jammed the iron lifter into the thick black plate to open the hole for the fuel. *Good. Still embers from breakfast.*

She hated it when the fire died and she had to start from scratch. It took too long. Dinner was to be served promptly at noon. Supper at six. She mustn't delay her father from his work.

How many times had she heard "*I have mouths to feed*"?

That meant Addie had mouths to feed. Today many more than she'd ever had. Twenty-three in all. Two Steins and twenty-one Germans. Her mother would not sup with the enemy; refused to be a part of this absurd situation. Despite Father's blustery wrath, Mother had packed up and caught a ride to Loveland. In spite of her mother's rampages, Addie had never before known her to go to Grandmother's as a result of an argument with Father.

Secretly, Addie admired her for standing up to him. Yet, that meant the burden fell to Addie. She hadn't had to fix extra breakfasts this morning because the Germans had arrived at seven. Tonight the prisoners would sleep in the hayloft, so that meant three meals tomorrow. She would have to get up at four to milk Bessie and Clarabelle.

Now almost noon, she'd been pumping water into the sink, cleaning, peeling, and baking for several hours, and she was already tired. *What will I be like at the end of the week?*

A knock at the kitchen screen door jarred her from speculation. The face of the enemy with the searching blue eyes peered through the screen. "*Herr* Stein tell me help *mit . . .* tables."

Addie's mouth went dry. She was angry at the intrusion— and at the leap of her heart. Without a word, she untied her apron and slammed out the door. In a huff, she arrived at the tool shed where she pointed to sawhorses, three long planks, then to a shady spot at the side of the barnyard under a mammoth oak tree. While the soldier set up makeshift tables, Addie upended buckets. She instructed the war prisoner to lay boards across them. Twelve-inch-wide lumber would provide seating. It would be a tight fit, but they were the enemy. Addie was sure they hadn't given even this much kindness to their victims. Nazis probably didn't serve *their* POWs three times a day.

From the corner of her eye, she noticed Father watching from the edge of the field. Glad she hadn't looked at or talked to the young German, she hurried toward the house. Standing on the porch where her father could still see her, she gestured inside, ordering the soldier to carry the kitchen table outside for a serving station.

"Fritz."

Startled, Addie whirled around.

"Fritz," the German repeated, pointing to himself.

Addie felt her face flush. "Then take these out and set them on the table." She made a sweeping gesture to glasses, cups, and silverware, plus roaster pans on the tall black-and-silver-plated cook stove. As well, she motioned to the mish-mash of plates stacked on the counter. Nothing matched. She had extracted every possible eating platter from the kitchen cabinets and had come up with only eighteen plates. Chipped, cracked, and otherwise. The rest of the prisoners would have to eat from pie tins.

With his arms bracing the upended table, Fritz backed through the screen onto the porch. Addie ran from the room.

Before her bedroom mirror, she was mortified at the coal dust streaked across her cheek. She poured water from a pitcher into a bowl. Splashing her face, Addie was able to cool the heat of the moment. After rearranging her hair into a bun at the nape of her neck, she returned to the kitchen.

With a glance out the window, she saw the error of her ways. Men stood around the crude temporary table and benches—waiting.

"Addie! Addie! We haven't got all day." Even from the house she could see that vein protruding on Father's forehead.

She checked to make sure Fritz had carried out all three pots of roast beef and potatoes and the kettle of gravy. Hurriedly, Addie took her place behind the serving table. As the men approached, she dispensed either a spoon or fork to each. They could not have both. Nor could they have milk for this meal. Water would have to do. By the end of the week, there would be no more of last year's potato crop. Mother would be furious.

Fritz reached toward her hand for his spoon. Instinctively, Addie pulled back. Her stomach flip-flopped at her reaction. She had already offered silverware to the other prisoners. Fritz was no different than any of them. She was irritated at the irritation this one German stirred within her. At once, her father was at her side.

"There a problem here?" He drilled a gaze into the Nazi.

Blood thrummed in Addie's ears. "It's just that this spoon is dirty." She snatched up the hem of her apron and thumbed the tableware.

Grabbing the utensil from her, Papa thrust it against Fritz's chest. "Dirty is as dirty does. Only reason I'm feeding you is to get work out of you. Now move along." Father shoved Fritz forward and glared at her.

Addie felt heat rise to her face. Only this time it felt different—like shame. Fritz hadn't done anything wrong. At least not today. She was confused. Why should she want to defend an enemy?

More than once during dinner, Addie felt Fritz's eyes studying her. When certain he wasn't looking, she stole glances at him.

At supper it was the same.

Lying awake in bed at the end of the long day, Addie pictured the German's countenance. His eyes seemed kind. Surely he had never killed. His smile offered warmth. His movements were helpful and gentle, not threatening. Rolling over, she squeezed her eyes shut against the image. She mustn't think untrue things. He was the enemy and a prisoner of war because he had killed defenseless Jews. Some even talked of women and children being killed. "Gassed," they'd said. Addie turned over again, away from things her mind refused to believe.

She slept fitfully.

When the alarm rang its tinny clamor at four in the morning and stuttered to its final clang, Addie's head felt thick, and her arms and legs as heavy as brim-full cream cans. She forced herself to rise and dress quickly. Even though yesterday had been hot, this morning's air chilled her skin through her thin, gingham dress. She threw on an old sweater and dashed to the outhouse.

Finished there, she quickened her steps in the dark toward the coal shed. The scuttle filled, she latched the door shut and headed for the house. A noise to the right startled her.

"Help . . . you." The voice was familiar, yet alarming. "Please." A hand reached out of the darkness, took hold of the pail and lifted it from her.

Afraid to linger, Addie hastened toward light peeking from the back door.

Fritz followed her into the kitchen and immediately set about scooping clinkers from the cast iron stove.

Still frightened, now because of what Father would say or do, Addie grabbed a pot, lowered it into the sink basin and pumped water for all she was worth. Which, if her father caught them together, wouldn't be worth much. Her heart raced past her thoughts. She had to get the German out of her kitchen. Now. "Out!" She pointed to the screen door.

Fritz smiled, bowed, and left.

Minutes later, when her nerves were not so frayed, Addie wondered why Father didn't obey Mother as willingly.

* * * * *

After breakfast, looking out the window from the kitchen sink, Addie stiffened with fear at the sight of her father talking to Fritz. When Father turned and marched toward the house, she stopped breathing.

Inside the back door, he halted, clamped his arms across his coveralls.

Swallowing to unstick her tongue from the roof of her mouth, Addie willed herself to draw air.

"That Nazi's only one can speak English. He gets the other prisoners set up, he's to come back here and help." Father screwed his index finger into his ear. "Can't be wasting time waiting around for grub." He scraped brown wax from beneath his nail. "Can't abide not having bread, either." He bore an admonishing glare. "You know that."

Addie did know but she simply hadn't had time to bake. "Will biscuits do?"

"This time. Tomorrow, better be bread on the table." He tromped off. Small clumps of dirt dislodged from the treads of his boots, leaving a trail in his wake.

Addie held her tongue, grabbed a straw broom and swept the kitchen's uneven oak floor with maddening strokes. She wasn't sure what made her the angriest—having to get up even earlier in the morning to start the bread's yeast action, listening to her father talk to her the same way he treated her mother, or being assigned a man . . . their enemy no less . . . to get in her way.

* * * * *

By the time she finished washing breakfast dishes, Fritz was on his way back from the field. She watched him stride with confidence, his broad shoulders and strong legs making him look older than she had first guessed. Twenty maybe. As he neared, Addie's heart beat faster. She tried to take her eyes off his face. Handsome—unlike the local men. Kind eyes—the likes of which she'd never seen.

At the door he rapped lightly with his knuckles, even though she was sure he saw her at the sink only six feet away. *How in the world am I going to get through this?* As he stepped inside, she nodded to a gunnysack in the corner. "You can start by peeling the potatoes."

Fritz nodded in return, then surprised her with a question as he hoisted the burlap bag onto the table. "How many years you have?"

"Years?"

"Seventeen." He tapped fingers on his chest. "You?"

Addie blinked. Surely he wasn't saying he was only seventeen. "You mean how old am I?"

"*Ja.*"

"Sixteen." She laid a paring knife beside potatoes spilling from the sack. *Is it safe to give him a weapon?* She eyed a butcher knife on the counter. Shaking off the possibilities, Addie argued, "You aren't seventeen."

"*Ja*. Seventeen." He held up all ten fingers, folded them into his palms, then raised five fingers on one hand and two on the other. "Ten *und* seven."

"How many men have you killed?" The moment the words came out of her mouth, Addie tensed at the question. Maybe that's what had been bothering her. She had to know.

"Me . . . *nein* kill."

"Nine?" The answer, like a dagger, penetrated her gut. She staggered backwards, gripped the counter's edge.

"*Nein* kill." Fritz shook his head while holding up both hands, fingertips circled to meet each thumb.

Swallowing a musket-ball-sized lump in her throat, Addie grasped for the truth. "Zero? None?"

"Iss so."

Blood rushed to her face in relief.

"Dis farm, like mine." Fritz gestured out the window.

"You live on a farm?"

"*Ja*. In Germany."

"What do you grow?"

"Many sings."

"Sings, huh? Like songs? You grow songs." Addie laughed at the thought of music sprouting out of the ground.

"*Nein* songs." Fritz thrust his tongue to the top of his teeth and forced a thick "th". Still, it came out "Sthings."

Addie giggled at the effort but stopped herself short, lest she silence him. She wanted to know more. How many in his family? What did he hope to do after the war? Did he have a girlfriend back home? At that question, Addie checked herself. Why should she care if he had a girlfriend? But already, she knew, her emotions were sneaking down a forbidden path.

The morning flew by as Fritz told of his little sister and how she loved to follow him around. He spoke of his dog—no, not a German shepherd—named, as best as Addie could translate, Brownie. Tears filled Fritz's eyes as he talked of his grandparents—his *Oma* and *Opa*. At this, Fritz shifted the conversation back to Addie. She was glad of it, for she could hardly stand the sadness in his face. Soon, they were laughing over his attempts to teach her a song and at her efforts at pronunciation.

The kitchen filled with gaiety, which was strange because gaiety was not often a visitor in this room. She had not known such companionship. At the end of the day, after two cooking sessions with Fritz, she glowed from the energy surging within her. Although far from tired, she could hardly wait to go to bed so morning would hurry and arrive.

*****

Scurrying about the kitchen, Addie glanced again and again out the window into the dim light of dawn. Where was Fritz? Had she said or done something to put him off? At the thought, her stomach rolled. Running every minute of yesterday through her mind, Addie examined and re-examined where she might have messed up.

The screen door squeaked. Her stomach flipped.

Fritz brushed by, barely touching her arm. Electricity charged through her. Had he meant to touch her? *Maybe . . . an accident.* Regardless, the effect was the same.

"You're late." Instantly, she regretted her words. She hated sounding like her parents.

"Sleep much." Fritz rubbed his eyes.

A sigh escaped Addie's lips.

The morning sped by. The afternoon went even faster. Addie wanted to stop time—to hold it in her hands and tuck these once-in-a-lifetime moments away in her heart.

Throughout the next week, every day enchanted Addie and thrilled, yet tormented her. For the first time in her life she actually came alive. *Is this what it's like to be in love?* If so, she wondered if her mother had ever experienced this.

Watching the sugar beet fields draw near to proper thinning, Addie dreaded the inevitable. Her chest grew heavy, as if a stone slab pressed upon her heart. It was hard to carry out daily tasks through tears swamping her eyes. After tomorrow, she would never see Fritz again. She didn't know what dying was like, but it had to be easier than this. Tomorrow meant goodbye forever.

* * * * *

Lying in bed listening to blood thrum in her ears, Addie heard someone at her open window.

Fritz whispered for her to join him.

She shook her head.

"Please." He offered his hand to help her out. "Iss safe."

She hesitated, then told him to wait. She shooed him away before stepping into her closet to dress. After crawling out the window, Addie stole away with him to the haystack on the other side of the barn. A crescent moon and the Milky Way dimly lit and webbed the sky.

Am I dreaming?

Fritz extended his palm to help her climb into the hay.

She drew back, refusing his offer.

Once they were both settled, he leaned forward and said, "I am glad for your company." His warm breath caressed her forehead. The exhilaration of it lifted her to startling heights.

This was nothing like Benjamin's awkwardness after the town social.

Addie sucked in her breath, pulled back.

As if discerning her innocence, Fritz turned his face toward the sky.

Immediately, Addie felt free to trust him. She heard his heavy sigh, sensed his will for self-discipline. Silence and stillness filled their time and space.

Addie wondered if his heart was beating as wildly as hers. Tears of joy, tears of sorrow, threatened to spill from her eyes.

They talked far into the night.

Her heart full, her eyes heavy, before she fell asleep, she told herself this innocent encounter would be enough to last a lifetime.

* * * * *

Just before dawn, Addie crept back into the house, went to her bedroom to pluck hay from her hair, then to the kitchen to prepare the final breakfast. The army truck would arrive at seven o'clock to take the prisoners to the next county.

As the rising sun spilled orange across the eastern skyline, Addie heard a vehicle door slam. Her mouth went dry. The transport was too early! She would not have this one last morning with Fritz. She found it difficult to breathe as she watched the Germans pile into the back of the army truck. Finally, filling her lungs with air, she sneaked out the back door and ran along the fenceline to the other side of the barn. There, she clambered up the wood ladder into the hayloft. Peering out the loft window, she searched frantically for Fritz's face among the mass of bodies as the vehicle crept out of the barnyard and rolled down the dusty driveway. She had to see him one more time. She must imbed his face in her mind forever.

A hand rose into the air in the middle of the troop. Fritz waved.

He sees me! Addie lifted her hand. In the yard below, Father turned to look up. Addie ducked and fell back onto the hard floor. Pain shot through her body. But the loss of her once-in-a-lifetime love hurt far greater than the throbbing from her fall. She crawled to where she imagined Fritz had slept in the hay and wept uncontrollably, yet silently. She would not allow her father any portion of what she and Fritz shared.

Addie poured out her grief. Finally exhausted, she made her way down from the loft and out of the barn to the well. She pumped cold water into her hands and washed her face. The cool liquid soothed the stinging in her eyes. In the field beyond the barbed wire fence, Addie saw her father tinkering with his tractor. Thankful for the solitude, she trudged to the house. Despite despair, she set to work in the kitchen.

"I see you got along just fine without me."

Startled, Addie saw the neighbor's car leaving the barnyard. Addie swung around to see her mother at the door examining the piles of clean dishes lining the countertop.

"We managed."

"We?" Mother raised an eyebrow.

Immediately, Addie knew her mother would know the "we" would not have included Father—not in the kitchen, anyway. "One of the prisoners helped me."

Mother snorted disgust as she plunked her suitcase on the floor.

"He was nice." Addie felt conflicted. She did not want her love for Fritz to be a secret, for then it would be as if it never were. Still, to share it would allow her mother to soil it.

Mother's eyes studying her, Addie turned, picked up the paring knife, and began peeling a potato. Fritz had liked her hash browns. His eyes had wrinkled into smiles at first taste. She hummed the song he'd taught her.

"Where did you learn that tune?"

"From a farmer who grows songs."

"What?"

"How was Grandma?"

"Same as ever."

"The man that helped me in the kitchen"—Addie drew a breath of courage.

"You mean the German prisoner?"

Addie ignored her mother's inability to understand that Fritz was more than that. "He never killed anybody."

"Is that what he told you?" Mother placed her hands on Addie's shoulders and turned her around.

Recognizing her mother's raised eyebrow as reprehension, Addie closed her eyes, picturing Fritz, that teasing twinkle in his eyes. From the place where she'd stored memories, she plucked an image of him—serious and sincere. Basking in the recollection, Addie mentally left the kitchen, if only for the moment.

"He didn't try anything with you, did he?"

Wrenched from her reverie, Addie's mind scrambled to hold on to the fading image. Addie picked up another potato. "It's not what you think." She wondered if Mother could ever comprehend a relationship based upon friendship and mutual respect. "A man can do what's best for the one he loves," she said just above a whisper.

Her mother's eyes strayed to the window and looked into the distance. She sighed.

At that moment Addie knew she had gone places her mother would never go.

"GERMAN DESCENT"

1946
Des Moines, Iowa

On my way home from school a thought sprouts from nowhere, excites me. Despite my limp—a result of being hit from behind by a bicycle—I quicken my steps, spurred on by my rumbling stomach. I wish I were rushing home to Momma instead of to this other prospect. I would give anything for my mother to be waiting in the kitchen, just as she did since my first day of Kindergarten.

My mind hugs those years of skipping into the house to her smile, her squeezes, a glass of milk, and cookies—snickerdoodles or *lebkuchen*. I savor those magical moments with her. Even now my mouth waters at the recollection of her streusel cake's cinnamon-aroma greeting. But these memories will have to suffice, will need to be strong enough to overshadow the emptiness of this past year without her.

If it meant not ever dating, or not graduating from Des Moines High this year . . . or eating for two weeks, I would trade them all right this minute for one more day with you, Momma. The futility of these wishful thoughts triggers the tangle of desperation, hope, and dread I experienced upon offering every one of those things, and more, to God in an attempt to bargain for her life—right up to the end when tuberculosis strangled her final struggle to breathe.

Were it not for the possibility of discovery once I arrive home, I would avoid this haste toward an empty house. Tears mar my vision. I reach into my sweater pocket and pull out a handkerchief—Momma's hanky. The scent of her—gardenia— provokes a swell of familiar feelings. Comfort. Sadness. Delight. Emptiness. These emotions and others I know but do not have a name for, whirl like a tornado within me. Everything is a blur, insignificant, far-away. Against the sidewalk, my feet beat to a speedy yet stuttering rhythm, even though they do not seem to be a part of me. My nose inhales air my lungs crave, but what is the use of taking in something that has ceased to exist between me and my mother? There is no air between the two of us, only solid ground—literally and figuratively. *Her grave . . . suffocating—*

"Hello, Klaudia. What's your hurry on this fine day?"

My eyes track to the sound of Mrs. Houtz' voice and fix on a cloud of dust swirling at the base of the straw broom in the old lady's weathered hands. On any other day I would stop to chat, but at this moment I am not a millionaire of time. "Got lots to do," I reply. Out of courtesy I raise my hand. It, too, is distant, not connected to me.

"Well, then, give your papa my regards." Mrs. Houtz resumes sweeping the porch where she and Momma spent many summer evenings—swaying back and forth, conversing back and forth—on a porch swing that now sits empty and idle. I wonder if it feels as abandoned as I do. I shake off my mental wandering, and realizing I have slowed my pace, pick it up.

Next door, I dash into my house, and am already at the top of the basement steps before I hear the slap-slap of the wooden screen door behind me. My leg warns me to take the stairs slowly. At the bottom of them, I wave my hand in the air, searching for the string of the overhead bulb. Click. Hair-like filaments flicker to life before an explosion of brightness assaults my eyes. I do not wait for them to adjust to the dim cement room. My arms out in front as battering-rams and shelf-detectors, I slide my feet, first the right, then the left, toward the far corner and a row of shelves. I am disgusted that the light dangling near the stairwell wastes all its power on such a small radius. On the other hand, I identify with the 25-watt bulb's limitations when I compare the energy I have now to the amount I had when Momma was alive.

I palm along a shelf and come away with a thick layer of dirt and the corpse of a beetle. The hand raised to Mrs. Houtz, which minutes before was not a part of me—the same one that now clutches death—refuses to detach from my body. Neither will the cadaver release its hold when I open my fist to dump it. *Is Momma's body this stiff and brittle?*

I reel backwards. The heel of my foot comes down on something small and cylindrical, causing it to spin beneath my weight. My arms windmill for balance. After I steady myself, I kneel to identify the culprit rolling away. A wood dowel, broken off of my mother's clothes-drying rack, revolves to a stop. *Will I ever get our clothes as clean as you did, Momma?* I suck in a breath, not so much for the oxygen, but to draw in the knowledge that, even in menial chores, what my mother did was right and good.

The room, heavy with her absence, presses in on me. I close my eyes, squat down. Pain shoots from my hip. Arms over my head, I bury my face between my knees. The whisper of air going in and out of my mouth sounds strange. I would rather this life-giving element be spent in dialogue with my mother.

I never thought about that before—that spoken words cannot exist without air.

As I open my eyes, I see the dowel pointing at me. Taking hold of it, I appreciate what a lifesaver the drying rack is in winter, when frozen air prohibits hanging laundry outside on the clothesline. I envision Momma touching this rung in my grip. I feel her energy, as if she is passing the baton, just as my twin brother Steffen does in his track team's relay race. I am charged with encouragement to keep going.

Tap. Tap. Tap. With the rod in my hand, I sweep side to side the shelves' dark recesses, listening for the clink of wood on glass that will announce a find.

Nothing.

Overturning a crate, I balance atop it, searching the top shelf—my last hope. I hold my breath. It does not help. I should have known Daddy would have found food if it were here.

Check beneath the stairwell.

Where does this thought come from? From hunger? Perhaps it is desperation shouting. Or could it be . . . ? I want to believe it is the sweet sound of Momma's voice, even though I know she cannot speak to me from the grave. I hop off my perch and scurry to the black space under the stairs. I see the dim outline of a cupboard, and feel along the front panel to a handle. I tug at the door's metal knob. It does not budge. I brace myself, wrap both hands around the knob and give a hefty yank. As the door gives way, I fall back onto a pile of junk—and spider webs. I spit the cobwebs out of my mouth, clawing them away from my face and out of my hair. I despise spiders—creepy, crawly, disgusting creatures.

My stomach growls, forcing me to acknowledge that right now hating arachnids is not top priority. What have they been guarding? Even though I cannot make out the cabinet's contents, I already feel the promising smoothness of glass, heavy in the lifting of one of Momma's canned goods. Sauerkraut? Wax beans? Beets? Maybe tomatoes, corn, or plum jelly. I cross my fingers. *Please, let there be apricots.* My mouth fills with saliva.

I gather three quarts in the crook of one arm, then carefully tuck two pints in the other before heading upstairs. In the kitchen, I set the Mason jars on the table and hurry down the basement steps for more treasure. Then up to unload, and back down again to turn off the light. I have already tacked more onto the electric bill than Daddy can pay. Taking the stairs to the kitchen two at a time, I suddenly have more strength than I have had in a month of Sundays. Soon, my stomach will not touch my backbone. I can hardly wait for that. And for the look on Daddy's face—Steffen's, too. Tonight we will dine on peas. Tomorrow on carrots. The day after that, green beans. We will save the apricots for after church.

Washing dust off the jars at the sink, I look out the window and see Daddy shuffle up the sidewalk. A few years ago, he did not walk like that. *A year ago, tuberculosis had not taken Momma and three years before that Hitler was not a household name—at least not in our home.* Within that span of time, neighbors gave up their sons to the guns of German Nazis and Daddy lost his job. Now, even though the war is over—at least overseas—here nobody will hire a *Kraut,* whether they give that as the reason or not.

Today, Daddy looks especially weary. His shoulders slump; he rubs a hand over his eyes. I have never known him to cry. I have never known him to hang his head, either. *Just watch, he will walk through that door as if all were right with the world.* Sure enough, Daddy pushes through the back porch door, his shoulders squared, his head high, and a smile on his face. His eyes widen at the harvest of jars. "Vat iss dis?"

"Supper!" I throw my arms around his thick chest and nestle my face into his starched shirt. Daddy insists on starch in his shirts to make a clean, crisp impression on prospective employers.

"Vere you get dese?"

"Underneath the basement stairs. Momma must have put them there." At the catch in Daddy's chest, I tighten my squeeze around him.

* * * * *

Tonight we ate the last of the canned goods. *Thank you, Momma, for two good weeks of meals. I miss washing dishes with you.* We always took turns washing and drying. I have kept track, and tonight would have been my turn to wash. Instead, I will wash and dry. Daddy and Steffen push back their chairs and go to the living room. I run hot water—but not too much—into the dishpan without the luxury of soap. When I turn off the faucet, I hear Steffen continue the argument he abandoned during dinner.

"Then I'll quit school and get a job," he says. Even though I cannot see him from here at the kitchen sink, I know his arms are crossed and his hands are tucked into his armpits.

"Und how vill you get job ven I cannot? Ve haf same last name. Bienhoff iss same for you as iss for me." In my mind's eye I see Daddy in his rocker staring at Steffen.

I put down the dishrag and go to the living room door. I am right on both counts—Steffen hugs his chest while Daddy glares.

Steffen and I have talked this over. It is now or never. In spite of Daddy's resistance, I know it has to be done. I swallow fear and cough up courage. I am startled at the sound of the discharge of air from my throat and am catapulted into a graphic image.

Coughing. Incessant coughing that spews blood. Momma's blood.

I am engulfed in a sea of red. I close my eyes to draw a curtain on the crimson drama. The inside of my lids mutate into scarlet reflectors. Tuberculosis attacks, hurling vivid scenes at me of its violence against my mother. Through a fog, I hear choking sounds.

"Klaudia, vat iss matter?"

I clear my throat, resisting these incinerating memories. "We are changing our names." There. It is out. I cannot make my eyes focus on Daddy. Perhaps if I get comfortable. I cross the room and drop into Momma's overstuffed chair. No one speaks. It is as if my words vacuumed air from the room. My heart beats against my ribs, but they are bars, imprisoning the organ pumping blood to my head. My face is hot. I am suddenly ashamed. Not of being German, but of hurting my father. *Would Momma be ashamed of me?*

"Und, vat you mean *change* name?" Daddy sounds old, weak, wounded.

His words are like a dagger in my chest. My heart leaks tears. I am glad heaven shields Momma from our grief—not just at this moment, but in the season of Hitler's evil reign that, even though he is dead, still casts a spell of darkness over Germans in America and everywhere on the face of the earth.

Steffen interrupts my thoughts. "Dad, it is not your doing that our milk bottles are empty and our cupboards bare." He walks to the door, kneels and picks up Daddy's shoes.

Our clock's little bird cuckoos six times, sending miniature milkmaids frolicking in a circle in and out of a tiny door. These same maidens danced for Momma as she crocheted doilies, darned stockings, and read her Bible every night. I am suddenly struck by the realization that this clock also ticked away the last minutes of her life.

Daddy fixes on the timepiece as well. I wonder if he is momentarily home again in the Black Forest. No one speaks until the maidens finish their frolic and the music dwindles to a stop.

Steffen holds the shoe in the air; his finger sticks through a ragged hole in the sole. "Job hunting has only earned you this," he says. "Now it is my turn to look for work."

"You are German. No one vill hire you, Steffen."

"Steve."

"Vat?"

"I am now Steve."

"Und, vat of your family name?"

"I'll go by my middle name. People will know me as Steve Alexander."

"And I am Claudia with a 'C'."

"Am I to be shamed . . . my own daughter vork to support her papa?"

"There is no shame in being a governess. I start next week for the Smiths, taking care of their two children after school."

Daddy's shoulders droop. He stares at the floor.

* * * * *

With the Smith children at their grandma's this afternoon, I cannot help but calculate the loss of the fifty cents I would otherwise earn for taking care of Judy and David. Still, I am glad for an opportunity to spend time with my brother. Out doing errands, we walk down Locust Street.

Steve clutches our white-rolled butcher package under his arm. He would rather have roast, as liverwurst is not his favorite, but I will spread it thin on the crusts of discarded bread I bring home from the Smiths and make it last through the week. After visiting Gustav's Butcher Shop, Steve has enough left of his first paycheck of seven dollars and thirty-eight cents—I think of this amount in spelled out terms in order to imagine it stretching farther than $7.38—to pay the water bill, which comes every three months. "By Divine intervention," as Daddy said, we are lucky our water was not shut off since we did not have enough money to pay the last bill.

"Nobody could prepare a rump roast like Momma." Even now I can smell the meaty fragrance wafting from her stove. I practically drool at the thought of her stew. I swallow the temptation to return to the butcher shop to spend the water bill money for a meal of beef. *Oh well, we could not have gravy without water, anyway.*

At the corner of 10th and Locust, we turn into the Masonic Temple Association Building and head for Des Moines Water Works. Steve digs in his pocket and pulls out six dollars and sixty cents. At the counter, he plunks it down.

A clerk—who looks like she just graduated high school— smiles at him. I cannot tell if her eyelash flutter is an attempt at a wink or if she has a nervous condition.

"This is for the bill we got yesterday . . . and for the one before that," Steve explains.

"Did you bring the bills with you?" The clerk flashes a glistening, toothy smile.

Steve sets the wrapped liverwurst on the counter and digs in both pockets. "Guess I forgot 'em." He shrugs. "Sorry."

"Not to worry," she coos. "The address?"

"59 Bowdoin."

"Name?"

"Steve."

She giggles. "And I'm Emily." Her eyelashes flit like butterfly wings. "What name is your billing under?"

Steve hesitates. Smiles for the first time. He is doing his best to head her off, but I know that in the time it takes him to close his lips after the "f" at the end of our last name she will shoot him down.

He hesitates. There is nothing else he can do—if we want water at home—but tell her. "Wolfgang Bienhoff."

Poof. Her teeth vanish behind lips that suddenly pinch off this budding relationship. She looks at the pad in her hand. With a quick scrawl and an ink-red "paid" slammed from a stamp in her other hand, she shoves the receipt at Steve.

Pink blotches spread like burns around his neck and throat and flare up his face. He pockets the abruptly offered receipt and turns on his heel for a quick exit. I am not so fast. I linger to glare at The Former Flirt, and stiffen as if to stifle the current of charges against our heritage.

* * * * *

"Please, Claudia," nine-year-old Judy pleads.

"Yeah, please, Claudia," David, seven, begs.

I move my finger down the page of the spelling book in my hands. "One more word. Premonition."

Judy sounds it out. "Prem-o-ni-tion." She gazes at a spot on the ceiling, as if the word is written there, and begins to spell. "P-r-e-m-i-n . . . No, wait. Let me start over. P-r-e . . . m . . . o . . . n . . . i . . . t-i-o-n. Premonition."

"Correct."

"Okay, now can we have some?" Judy jumps up.

"All right. But *after* you do the rest of your homework." I love these kids. It is nice to come to a house with laughter—and life. Judy and David are happy. Normal and naïve. They do not know there was a war in Germany, nor that I am German. If they do, it must not matter to them. They hug me around the waist then scamper off to the den to tackle arithmetic problems in order to earn a dish of homemade lemon-custard ice cream.

I take pride in Judy's spelling development and love grilling her on words every night after school. I am pretty sure that is why she is in the Regional Spelling Bee tomorrow. Being governess is the next best thing to actually being a teacher. Even if I save every penny for the next five years, I still will not be able to afford college. Besides, there is no saving. Except for saving face by paying the electric bill and buying a few groceries. I am not as hungry now because I can have all I want to eat here, but for some reason I am skinnier than I have ever been. Momma would croak at how my once stylish dresses hang on me. *At least she would if she were not already dead.*

I hate it when thoughts like that pop into my head. They are not the least bit funny and they make me feel guilty. Why does guilt bully someone who is already full up with grief? Why should I feel guilty about how I feel about Mrs. Smith? Is it wrong to miss Momma and love Mrs. Smith at the same time? Mrs. Smith is a professional woman—a doctor just like her husband. I can only imagine how smart she must be. And how much courage it takes her to work in a man's profession. I know she is brave because sometimes after the Smiths get home from their hospital rounds, I overhear them talking. From what I can make out, it is difficult for Mrs. Smith to work with a bunch of men who think they have all the answers in the world.

The kids break into my woolgathering when they yell from the den. "We're done!"

"Come and get it," I call back from the kitchen.

David skids around the corner and slides across the linoleum floor. Judy is right behind. They sidle up to the table where ice cream begins to melt in their bowls.

"Yummy." Cream drips down David's chin.

"Read to us, Claudia." Judy swipes her mouth with the back of her hand. "You're right to the part where Laura heard a roar in the chimney. Remember?"

David stops scooping. "Yeah, and you said 'What if it's a chimney fire?' What if it is, Claudia? Will it burn their log house down?"

He looks so serious I cannot help but laugh. "We will just have to find out." I leave them with orders to not make a mess while I go upstairs to get *Little House on the Prairie* from Judy's room. Climbing the steps, I hear voices; I had not heard the Smiths come in. Going down the hallway, I pause beside their half-open bedroom door when I hear my name.

The tone of Mrs. Smith's voice catches me off guard. "Roger, the children love Claudia, and so do I." She pauses, and I detect the padding of her feet crossing the carpet. I dare to peek through the narrow slit in the door where it is hinged to the frame and see Mrs. Smith standing at the window. When she speaks, it is toward the pane. "I don't care what the Chief of Staff says. It is none of his business."

Mr. Smith snorts. "Mary, it's not worth it. Surely you can find another teen. It's not like they're at a premium around town."

"Dr. Jones is a bigot. His prejudice sickens me." Mrs. Smith sounds like she might cry.

"Granted, but he is unprecedented in procuring donations for the Hospital Foundation. The wing you work in is his baby. The Board loves him. Administration loves him."

"But to call us Nazi sympathizers simply because we employ a German girl, and for him to insist on us getting rid of her because it might *tarnish* the hospital's public relations? That is ludicrous!"

This is like the time in fifth grade when Danny Bolis punched me in the gut. I cannot breathe. My head is hot and swells with stuff that clogs my ability to think—or act. My mouth dries up. The room spins around me. My legs wobble. I lean against the wall and slide to the floor. All of a sudden, Mr. and Mrs. Smith are standing over me as I gasp for air through sobs. I was not aware of the noise that alerted them to my presence. *Is this what Momma felt like in her last minutes . . . not being able to breathe?* For the first time, I think maybe tuberculosis is not the cruelest form of death. At least when TB choked life from Momma, it put her out of her misery— and she got to go to heaven where nothing or nobody will ever cause her pain again.

Mrs. Smith kneels and reaches to wipe tears from my cheeks. I let her. "Oh, honey, I'm so sorry you had to hear that." The touch of her cool hand against my burning face feels reassuring.

Mr. Smith backs up and props his hands behind him against the stair rail. "Claudia, we have no other choice."

I want to get up and run but I do not trust my legs. I look at Mrs. Smith, knowing she will stand up for me. She will not allow Mr. Smith to decide this. After all, she knows all about discrimination. Maybe not from a German's standpoint, but certainly from a woman's. I wait, expecting. She does not speak. Instead, she pulls me into her lap and breathes warm air on the top of my head. This feels like love. I do not understand how she can use air for love but not for words.

It is awkward, my departure. I am not sure how I make it down the stairs, to the kitchen, past the children, and out the door. It is all a haze, as if it cannot be real.

It is only when I bury my head into my feather pillow in my own bedroom that I am aware of my body. I am clammy from the sweat of limping home as fast as I could, damp from tears streaming from my swollen eyes, drenched from fear seeping from every pore in my skin, and flooded with the searing heat of shame.

I sense Daddy beside my bed, then feel the weight of him sitting on the edge of the mattress. Feel his hand caress my hair. Feel his warm breath as he kisses the top of my head. Feel the heaviness in his heart. *This* is love.

For a long time, we say nothing. There is no need to. Both of us know and understand.

Finally, I roll over and stare at the ceiling. "I do not want to be German. I did not ask to be German. I hate being German. I hate Hitler and am glad he is dead. I hate the Hospital Chief." I bend my arm over my eyes.

Daddy sighs.

Steve enters the room. "What's cookin'?"

"Hatred," Daddy answers. "Iss boiling over." He pats a spot beside him on the patchwork quilt. "Sit, Steffen. Iss like poison."

"What's like poison?" Steve asks.

"Hatred."

"I'll say," Steve agrees. "Gushes out of idiots like sewage. Being treated rotten because we're German, stinks."

Daddy shakes his head. "Iss not about being German."

From under my arm I see Steve squint his eyes, wrinkle his forehead. His mouth pinches up, scrunches his nose.

"If it vas about being German, den Hitler vould not have killed Germans," Daddy says, rubbing the heel of his hand on his knee.

I do not understand. "But Hitler was German," I say.

He killed Jews," Steve adds.

"Vell, der are German Jews. Und dey ver not da only victims. Vat about da Polish? Und Gypsies. Und political dissenters?" Daddy rises and crosses the room to stand at the window. For a long while, he stares outside, as if examining the world. At last, he speaks, "No, hatred does not discriminate. Und iss not one-sided."

Steve repeats, "Not one-sided?"

Daddy turns, his eyes filled with tears. "Hatred destroys vessel iss poured *into*, und iss pouring *out* of vessels now in dis room."

It is true. Hatred's poison surges through my body, soul, and spirit. Momma appears in my imagination and beckons me to a time when a neighbor was especially hateful. Momma responded in kindness, refusing hatred to be poured into her. Suddenly, I know what she meant about kindness being a shield—and forgiveness a wrapper. But then, Momma did not have to endure what the three of us are going through. This is different.

Without further discussion, Daddy leaves the room. Steve flops back, his arms extended over his head. I pull up my feet to make room for him at the end of the bed. I do not want to think anymore. My head hurts. My whole body hurts. It hurts to live. Momma is the lucky one. Daddy comes back into the room. He offers envelopes to us.

"Your Momma pen a letter to each of you. She said I vould know ven to give."

I sit up, prop a pillow behind me. I connect with a rush of excitement, sadness, and anticipation as I take the envelope. Opening it, the fragrance of gardenia wafts up. I can hardly breathe as I begin to read.

> My Dearest Klaudia,
>
> How I wish I could be there with you at this moment. However, God had other plans for me, just as He must have for you right now.
>
> Because Papa gave this to you, you must be struggling with something bigger than yourself. This is actually a good thing, as trials give birth to perseverance. Perseverance produces character. The fruit of character is hope.
>
> When you embrace the truth of this and wrap yourself in forgiveness, you can conquer whatever problem you face. Then you will be free to live in peace . . . peace that will guard your heart and your mind.
> All My Love,
> Momma

I reread her letter. Read it again. Trace my finger over her beautiful handwriting, drink in the floral fragrance of her scent. I was wrong—spoken words *do* exist without air.

I breathe in Momma's desire for my peace and resolve to step onto the path that will lead me there.

"SMOKIN' 'EM"

August, 1946
Farmstead Outside Fargo, North Dakota

"Ya got the goods?" Digger thrust his hand out, palm up.

"Yup. Three. Ma won't even miss 'em." Jonesy patted his chest pocket. "You?"

"Yep. Come up with a near-empty pack of the ol' man's." Digger shaded his eyes and looked across the pasture. "There's Ralph. Wonder how many he filched? Beings he's only eight and ain't none too bright, bet he don't got nothing." At ten years old, Digger considered himself experienced, and today's activity would add to his know-how. He jammed his hands deep into the pockets of his Oshkosh overalls, leaned back, and propped his shoeless foot against the weathered barn. "Here he comes."

The pals zeroed in on the small figure crossing the fenced field with strides almost larger than his legs allowed.

A gust of wind flattened the last of grass left from the summer's drought. Dark clouds hunched on the horizon of an otherwise blue sky.

Ducking between two middle strands of rusty barbed wire, Ralph darted behind the towering old barn and stopped just short of its shadow dominating the grounds. He surveyed to his left, then to his right.

"We ain't gonna get caught." Digger rubbed his tender backside, a result of his shenanigan yesterday of feeding his sister a tomato worm. It wasn't his fault she was stupid enough to believe it would taste like green candy. He nonchalantly screwed a finger into his nostril. Pulled it out. Examined it. Flicked a booger.

"If *your* Pa was a preacher, *you'd* be on the lookout, too," Ralph said, squinting against the afternoon sun. "Better be careful yourself. Filling your little sister's shoes with pig poop before church last week wasn't none too smart. Your ma said—"

"Yeah, yeah. I know what she said." Digger rubbed his other butt cheek in memory of the price he'd paid for the hog dung. "Ain't gonna be no trouble today. Ma and Pa drove the Studebaker into Fargo this morning for supplies, so ain't nobody home 'cept the little pest. I hate watching a five-year-old-mush-for-brains. Got better things to do."

Lightning flashed in the distance. A second later, thunder pushed past them. Overhead, the haymow door creaked ajar in the breeze. Jonesy backed out of the barn's shade and scrutinized the loft opening way up high. "Speaking of the brat, where is little-miss-perfect Alice?"

"In the outhouse. Reading the Sears and Roebuck Catalogue." Digger nodded toward the "sit shack," as he called it.

"Now I know you're lyin'." Jonesy sneered. "Alice don't read."

"So she's looking at the pictures. What's it to ya?" Digger's nose twitched, redirecting his attention. "Dagnabbit, Ralph, ya oughta watch where you step. Pee *you!*"

"Was in a hurry. Sorry."

Jonesy chimed in, "Well, hurry your sorry behind over to the water tank and get rid of that cow pie." He fanned his nose with dramatic flair.

Obediently, Ralph walked on his heels, toes spread, to the round metal container. Once there, he sat on its silver lip and swung his legs into the water. Three quick kicks sufficiently freed the manure. He rejoined Digger and Jonesy in his too-short raggedy pants—held up by a rope—now soaked to the patched knees. Flashing a toothy grin, he produced a packet from his shirt pocket. "Uncle Leonard's C-rations. From The War in Germany."

Digger spat, aiming for a beetle crawling over a dirt clod. "War's been over, over a year now. What's he saving 'em for? World War III?"

"He don't smoke no more." Ralph ran a grimy hand over his towhead crewcut.

"Seems like he don't do a lotta things no more." Digger snickered.

Ralph kicked at the dirt. Dust settled around his ankle and covered his foot with muck. "Yeah, well maybe he ain't exactly right in the head."

"So cough 'em up," Digger demanded. A flashbulb-second later, he slapped his knee. "Cough 'em up. Smokes. Get it? Har. Har. Har."

Ralph unwrapped the cellophane from the small, cardboard box and extracted its contents—four long, square-sided cigarettes. "Chesterfields."

"Whadda *you* got, Jonesy?" Digger pushed off the barn, stomping blood back into his tingling foot.

"Old Golds."

"Old Golds?" Digger said and spat again. "Women's smokes."

Jonesy's nostrils flared. "Yeah, well at least they're patriotic."

"How ya figure?" Digger crossed his arms over his chest, tucked fingers into his shirtless pits.

"During The War, they was the only ones advertised to back the attack and buy war bonds."

"Who says?"

"My Grandpa. That's who. And he knows about everything there is to know about anything." Jonesy spread his legs, stuck his chest out and planted his hands on his scrawny hips.

"If they're so patriotic, how come the Army packed Chesterfields?" Ralph tightened his jaw.

"Yeah, Jonesy," Digger said, propelling his index finger off Jonesy's bony collarbone.

Jonesy tottered back. "War's over, like ya said. I ain't gonna start another."

Digger relaxed his shoulders, pulled out a pack with a red circle on the front. "L.S.M.F.T. Lucky Strike Means *Fiiine* Tobacco."

"Fine tobacco, my hiney." Jonesy snickered. "L.S.M.F.T. Loose straps mean floppy Tetons." He flapped his hands over his chest and pranced around like a girl.

Digger laid into Jonesy. Ralph jumped back.

From the corner of Digger's eye he watched Ralph inch to the ground against the barn's red-paint-chipped boards. *Pantywaist. Soon as I get done bustin' Jonesy's chops, I'll knock some of that sawdust out from between Ralph's ears. Gotta get all the training in I can before I join up to be a soldier.*

When the dust cleared, Digger and Jonesy were coated with grime but no blood.

"If you guys are done messing around, let's get to what we came here for," Ralph said. "Where's the matches?"

Digger scrambled to his feet, dusted himself off. "If they was snakes, they'd a bit ya." He jerked his head toward a box of kitchen matches in a clump of withered weeds at Ralph's feet.

Swaggering over, Digger nonchalantly picked up the rectangular container and pushed the tray out just far enough to fetch a match. He folded his fingers around the stick. The red and blue nub peeked over his index finger. Hooking his thumbnail on top of the match head, Digger held his breath, then flicked fire to life.

"Wow," Ralph whispered.

A burst of air escaped Digger's lips. "Nothin' to it."

Jonesy jumped up. "Dirty rotten liar. Ya been practicing."

"So, what's it to ya?"

"Betcha can't do it again."

"Don't wanna. Here you try."

Jonesy crooked his fingers around the match, poised his thumb above the red gob, snapped his nail back. The stick broke. "Don't make 'em like they used to." He pulled out another. On the second try, a flesh-singeing flare sent Jonesy into a yowl.

"I don't have all day," Ralph said, poking one of the Chesterfields between his lips and the other three back in the pack. "Gotta be home by suppertime." He snatched a match, scratched it along the side of the box, raised it to his mouth. The flame burned into the tobacco. Ralph sucked short puffs.

"Ya ain't inhaling. Here, let me show ya how a real man does it." Digger tapped the Chesterfield pack on the side of his hand 'til a cigarette protruded. This time he swiped a match on the container's sandy strip and held the flicker to the fag. Taking a deep draw, he swallowed. Just as quickly, smoke billowed from his nostrils and mouth. A coughing fit broke out, sending Ralph and Jonesy into laughing fits.

Suddenly, the sky went dark. Lightning zigzagged close to the ground, splitting seams of storm clouds hanging low in the air.

All three boys rolled their eyes upward. An eerie silence almost swallowed their fun.

Jonesy, first to break the spell, wiped his nose on his bare arm. "Let *me* show ya how it's done." Puffing away, he inhaled, gulped, exhaled. Inhaled, gulped, exhaled. Plucked flecks of tobacco off his tongue between the tips of his thumb and finger.

Digger lit another. This time he was ready for the assault on his lungs. Now he had the hang of it. Smoke curled up into his right eye. He buttonholed his eyes like he'd seen Humphrey Bogart do on the big screen. Digger said a few words with the cig clinging precariously between his lips the way Bogie did in *Action in the North Atlantic.* Now, there was a sailor what knowed how to deliver the goods. Digger imagined himself a Merchant Marine, swaggered like one.

For the next several minutes, all three boys drew deep drags.

Suddenly, Digger didn't feel so good. "Dang, these are strong sons-a-guns. Must be accounta they're aged."

Ralph nodded. "Tobacco and wine get better with age."

"Who told you that bull puckey?" Jonesy squatted on his haunches.

Ralph clenched his teeth. "Everybody knows that."

"Knows what?" Alice skipped around the corner of the barn and skidded to a stop. Her eyes widened. "I'm going to tell Mommy on you, Digger."

"Go ahead, you little snot-nose snitch."

"I'm going to wait for her by the mailbox." Alice pivoted, spun out in the dirt.

"And I'll tell her you been playing with matches," Digger yelled. His cigarette lost its grip and plummeted to the ground.

Alice swerved to a halt. "Have not!"

Dizzy-headed, Digger sidled up to her. "Then what's this?" He poked his index finger through a burn-hole in the skirt of her cotton dress.

"Oooh! Get your snotty finger outta my dress." Alice jerked away and wheeled out of his reach.

Jonesy retched. Puke shot from his mouth like water from a hose. Only the stuff wasn't clear. Stench exploded like a hand grenade. Stink-shrapnel lodged in Digger's nostrils, pierced his eyeballs, drew tears. His stomach rolled. Then wrenched. Rolled. Wrenched. The barn moved. Ralph and Jonesy faded in and out.

Alice scrunched her nose. "Pee-yew!" She cut a hasty retreat toward the catch pen on the side of the barn before raising her voice to Ralph. "How come your face isn't green like Digger's and Jonesy's?"

"I'm not old enough to smoke," Ralph said, hiding his Chesterfield behind his back.

"Or dumb enough," Alice added, climbing to a top board of the corral where she teetered on her tummy across the rail. Her head upside-down, she peered between the planks. "Digger, I know you won't tell Mommy I was playing with matches."

The ground swelled beneath Digger's feet as he staggered toward his sister. "That's what you think."

"You won't because you was s'posed to be watching me."

"Why you little—" Digger lunged for Alice's leg.

Alice lost her balance and flipped over the rail, catching her skirt on a nail. *Riiippp.*

Ralph ran forward and caught her before she hit the ground.

Alice stared at the damage. "Looky what you did now, Digger. You tore my good dress. Mommy's gonna be real mad." She started to cry. "Maybe even mad at me."

Her wails were like fingernails on the blackboard of Digger's scruples, which Ma said he needed more of, but which he saw no need for. They only got in the way. Like now— because Alice only had one dress, her good one. He hated it when his conscience plagued him like this. It was a tussle, but he successfully wrestled free from it.

"Look, Alice. Your burn-hole is gone." Ralph pointed to the proof.

Without warning, lightning struck the rooster weather vane atop the barn.

All eyes turned to fix on the flash and the spinning, blackened rooster. But it wasn't the cock that commanded their attention. Digger's sour-tasting mouth dried at the sight. His stomach seized up, though not from the nicotine. What he saw loomed worse than anything happening in his body. Lots worse.

Smoke belched from the hayloft!

Not wasting a moment, he yelled at Jonesy and Ralph to grab milk pails from the barn. "Fill 'em with water from the tank! Alice, you, too."

Alice jumped off the fence and ran to Digger. "I didn't mean to. Honest. I didn't."

Digger elbowed her aside. Dashed for a pail. Dunked it into the water. Bolted for the barn. Scrambled one-handed up the ladder to the loft. Sprang onto the floorboards. Gained balance. Pulled back the bucket and swung it forward. Water arced through the air. Splashed on smoldering hay. He ran to the loft window, tossed the pail to the ground. Grabbed a rope, thrust it through the pulley hanging from the eve. Lowered the rope to the ground. "Jonesy, tie your bucket on. I'll hoist 'er up."

By now, Alice was in the loft at Digger's side. "I tried to find it. I did. You gotta believe me."

Digger shoved her out of the way and yanked on the rope, trying not to spill a drop of the life-saving liquid. Again, an arc of water. This time, the resulting puddle revealed a burnt match in the straw. Picking it up, he shifted his gaze to Alice. "Why, you little—"

Thunder clapped, rolled. Followed by a second ear-splitting explosion.

Alice burst into tears.

Digger didn't have time for this. After grabbing an armload of smoking hay, he sprinted to the loft door. "Look out below!" Again, another scoop of scorched hay.

"Heads up. Comin' at ya!" Several more trips, and several more buckets of water.

Finally, Digger eagle-eyed the remains. "Think we got it."

HONK. HONK. A truck door slammed.

Digger broke out in a sweat.

Ralph peeled out across the barnyard, under the fence, and across the pasture in a cloud of dust. "You can have the rest of the Chesterfields," he yelled over his shoulder. "Me and Uncle Leonard won't need 'em anymore."

Jonesy beat feet, as well, disappearing in the opposite direction.

Digger found himself looking down into Pa's angry face. Ma didn't look none too happy, neither. Especially when she spied the pack of cigarette butts on the ground and Ralph's half-empty pack of Chesterfield's in Pa's clenched fist.

Alice poked her head around Digger's leg. "Digger's sick."

Yeah, sick of getting smoked out in the open and being the butt end of a bum deal every time I'm minding my own business. Digger's thoughts sailed off across the ocean where he would join up with the Merchant Marines and become a hero. *Then they'll think twice 'bout treating me rotten. Better yet, I'll get killed saving the ship from getting blown up. When I come home dead* then *they'll all be sorry.*

"He's been—" Alice continued.

Digger broke her off, nudged her behind him, and spoke out the side of his mouth. "Shut up, ya little twerp. Let me handle this."

Pa glared up at him. "Smoking in the loft, were you? What kind of idiotic, stupid stunt—?" Pa kneeled down, examined the drenched, charred hay. "Get down here right now. You're going to get the butt beating of your short life."

Swallowing the rock of hard knocks in his throat, Digger knew he was in for it for sure. "I'll take the rap for smoking on the ground, but not for the fire up here," he whispered to Alice. As soon as the words were out of his mouth, he realized that would only rile Pa more. How did Bogie make the tough-guy voice work to his advantage?

Alice grabbed hold of his pants with a grip so tight it pinched his skin. Digger stink-eyed her puny face. Tears rolled down her grubby cheeks, forging a crooked, dusty-flesh-colored path to her chin. Her eyes showed fear he'd never seen before. *Scaredy cat. Lily-livered brat. Baby.* Baby. Yeah, she wasn't much more than a baby.

By now Pa was on the top rung of the ladder. Before Digger had a chance to think, the pounding of Pa's footfalls stopped dead, and Digger's overall suspenders ended up clenched in his ol' man's fists.

Thunder detonated. The blast brought Digger to his senses, clearing cobwebs from his head. Lightning streaked across the sky, unzipping water-laden clouds. The wetness of Alice's cheeks brushed against his arm, and her whimper soaked through his skin and seeped into his scruples.

"There's the culprit, Pa," Digger choked out, pointing to another bolt zigzagging in the heavens. "It's what started the fire up here. Ain't that right, Alice?"

Alice vigorously nodded her head. "Yeah, and that preacher's kid's the one brought over the cigarettes. Lookit him run away 'cause he knows he sinned." She aimed a finger at Ralph, a diminishing figure in the distance.

Digger was shocked at this. He certainly didn't know Alice knew about sinning. Maybe she wasn't such a baby after all.

"UPSTART OR NEW START?"

Late May, 1947
Henrieville, Utah

"Lloyd, it's nothing more than an upstart industry. There is no way on God's green earth this is here to stay. I don't think it's a good idea," Mom says in a huff.

Daddy sighs. "You worry too much. I'd welcome a little trust."

I don't exactly have to have my ear pressed to their bedroom door to hear them arguing. They've been at it for months. Even at twelve, I'm old enough to know Daddy is ready to sell everything and move to California to buy this new business. Since he lost his left arm in the War, he can't do diesel mechanic stuff anymore.

In fact, he doesn't do a lot of things he used to. Like joke around. Whistle little ditties while he works. Play baseball with me. Take me to stock-car races. Wrestle. Dance with me. Or smile, even. Daddy has a far-off look in his eyes. And he hardly ever looks *me* in the eye.

Grandma says it's because he lost something in France—besides a limb. "But don't you worry," she says, "all he needs is a chance to provide for his family."

I get tummy aches thinking about leaving Grandma and my friends. But I want my daddy to be happy. Then maybe he'll dance with me again. If moving will make that happen, it'll be worth it.

Finally Mom says, "Okay, Lloyd. If that's what you want, I won't stand in your way. You better just hope this doesn't wreck Maxine's life." I imagine Mom crossing her arms over her chest with her lips pinched.

Butterflies flutter in my stomach over this chance for Daddy to prove himself.

* * * * *

Yesterday, school got out for the summer. Today we're all packed and loaded in our DeSoto. I'm in the back seat squashed up against the window by boxes and suitcases. Grandma's standing on the curb, her hands on her hips. With her elbows sticking out like wings, she looks like a chicken. When I smile at her, her lips quiver. She unbuttons her dress at the neck and pokes her hand inside. She rummages around and hauls out a hanky. "I'll write to you, Maxine," Grandma promises.

"That'll be swell," I say. "Do you think I'm worth a three-cent stamp?"

Instead of laughing, Grandma yanks off her spectacles and busts out bawling. She sticks her head through my open window and grabs me around the neck. She whispers into my ear, "Sweet Cheeks, I'm going to miss your dimples."

"All right, that's enough caterwauling," Daddy says, swiping his good arm across his nose. "Goodbye, Ma. Okay, here we go!" He brackets his legs around the steering wheel while he shifts into reverse with his right hand. Then first gear. Shift. Second. Shift. Third gear. Daddy's got the moves down pat.

I watch out the rear window until Grandma is nothing but a speck.

"It's all going to work out fine. You'll see, Max," Daddy says.

Max. Daddy called me Max. He's never done that before. Maxine. Maxie. Maxazine. And Mix-and-Max. Never just Max. It makes me feel grown up—like I'm his buddy. From here on out it's going to be *Dad* and Max.

So long, Henrieville.

Nobody utters a peep for a stretch of miles. Except for Dad. Every now and then he says, "See, Eloise, there's one."

A batch of towns and the third motor court later, Mom snaps at Dad. "How many automobiles do you see parked at them, Lloyd?" I can't see Mom's hands from the back seat, but I know she's wringing them.

Dad's jaw tightens, along with his grip on the steering wheel's suicide knob. "That's because it's one o'clock in the afternoon. People don't stop till evening at a motor inn." He sucks in a gush of air. "Oscar and C.L. Tomerlin started theirs in 1930. Look where they are now—and in only seventeen years. They claim auto courts are the modern version of stagecoach inns." He gestures at the road ahead with his left hook. "With America's highways taking off—no pun intended—heh, heh, here's where our future lies." Dad glances in the rearview mirror and looks me dead in the eyes. He winks. "Out there is a miracle just waiting to happen," he says.

My heart jumps and pumps out warmth that oozes through my whole body. I lean back in the seat. My eyelids roll down like window shades.

* * * * *

When I wake up, the DeSoto is parked. An orange motel light lights up the front seat.

"We're here. The Starlight Motel in Burbank, California— our new home." Excitement springs from Dad's voice.

Mom tugs a couple of bobby-pins out of her red hair and slicks stray strands back. She pries the pins apart with her teeth, fastens them back into place. She swivels her head, looking the place over. "This is an oil spot in the road. No one will ever come here." She sighs.

I wonder how she can tell, beings it's nighttime.

Dad gets out, slams the door.

Mom stares straight ahead. She sighs again and bows her head.

Mom is praying? I can't believe it. Grandma's always trying to get Mom to go to church, but Mom'll have nothing of it. Before we left, Grandma told her, "All things work out for the best for those who love the Lord, Eloise." Mom took one look at Dad's hook and pressed her lips together so tight it looked like her mouth was a razorblade slit. Without all the bloody gore, of course.

I silently tack on to whatever Mom is asking right now. *Dear God, let this be the answer to Dad's prayers. And if you're really in a miracle mood, Mom needs all the help she can get. Amen.*

Dad comes out of the office whistling. He waves a paper in the air. "We're the proud new owners."

We unpack a few things and cart them in to the two bedrooms, dinky bathroom, kitchen-dining room combination, and what-there-is-of-it living room that is now our home.

The next morning, Dad plants his hand on my shoulder, looks me in the eyes and says, "Max, we're a team and you're almost a young lady now. Your job is to man the front desk and sign in lodgers." Suddenly, a wrinkle crawls across his forehead.

He raises his eyebrows to push it away. "Most customers will be nice, but you'll encounter some who will try to give you guff. Don't let them get away with it. Hold your ground, and they'll see you know what you're doing."

I can't let Dad down.

Everything ticks along like clockwork the first day. The second, and so on.

A few bumps in the road here and there with customers, but already we're into our second month of running this place.

One afternoon a man missing his right leg hobbles toward our office on crutches. I try not to notice, even though I see about everything through the big window in front of my desk. I sign the guy in and give him keys to the nearest room. A woman climbs out of the driver's side of the car and a boy about my age crawls out of the back seat. The man crutches out to the trunk of his banged up Hudson with his leg stub dangling. When he yanks out a suitcase it catches on something. He tumbles sideways and down he goes. His crutches clatter to the ground. The woman and boy scamper to help him.

The man yells not-so-nice words at his family and orders them to take their bags to Room 2.

With all the commotion, Mom comes out of the laundry. She glances at Dad who's at the end of the motel using his shoulder to prop up a board while he nails it down.

I'm sure as shootin' glad Dad doesn't yell at me.

Anyway, my job gives me time to read educational literature, like the Little Lulu comic book some kid left in Room 9 a coupla weeks ago. Dad calls the left-behinds one of the benefits of the job. So far, I've acquired a can of tooth powder; Poli-Grip for false teeth; a tube of fire-engine-red lipstick, which Mom won't let me wear 'til I turn sixteen; a

Zippo lighter; three combs; one hairbrush; and Mum cream deodorant, for when I start to sweat.

The best left-behind, though, is this nifty radio. Speaking of which, it's time to switch stations. I'm tired of listening to Frank Sinatra. I jimmy the knob to *The Green Hornet* coming on next. Britt Reid is my kind of hero. He has the flatfoots believing he's the mastermind behind all the crime. What they don't know is, during the day Britt is editor of the *Daily Sentinel*. At night he turns into the Green Hornet, Overcomer of Evil. He comes by his crime fighting naturally, beings he's the great-nephew of the Lone Ranger. Instead of a horse, G.H.'s Black Beauty is a high-powered motor car. I'm ready for a high-speed chase. Just have to get the station tuned in—"

DING! DING! DING!

"Say, Mister, what's the big idea dinging the bell? I'm right under your nose."

"I'm looking for Max."

"Yeah."

"The one-armed whistler out there says Max'll fix me up." Mister's Camel cigarette bounces up and down at the corner of his mouth. He takes off his brown felt hat and runs fingers through his greasy hair. "So, doll-face, ya gonna tell me where Max is, or are ya gonna stand there beatin' your gums all day?"

"I'm Max." I politely shove a 3 X 5 paper across the counter and tell him to write down the name of everybody staying in the room and his address.

"Whaddaya need my address for?"

"In case you lift anything—we'll know where to send the coppers. Ha. Ha." It hasn't taken me long to learn the lingo out here.

I read the names on the slip, then read them again, this time out loud. "*Tooter, Tink,* and *Tiny?*"

"Tooter's given to flatulence," says a little lady motioning toward the nincompoop in front of me as she flits through the door.

"She's nicknamed after Tinkerbelle," explains Tooter, snagging his arm around her dainty neck.

"So, who's Tiny?"

"Our son." Tooter and Tink point in unison toward a tree leaning against an Edsel parked outside.

I eyeball the three-hundred-pound, give-or-take-fifty, Tiny towering over the roof of the car.

"Just fix us up and don't give us any lip," Tooter says.

"Ease up, Tooter. She's just a kid," Tink says.

Tink's gotta be the brains of the bunch.

"May be, but she sure ain't as sweet as she looks. Them dimples are deceptive," Tooter says.

I fix 'em up all right. Put 'em in Room 4—where the bed springs sag and the window is painted shut. With Tooter's flatulence, Tiny might just be asphyxiated by morning. Tink, being a fairy, will most likely escape the fumes.

"That'll be ten dollars," I say.

"Highway robbery. You got some racket going here, kid," Tooter mutters.

"As a matter of fact, I do." I reach into my left-behind treasure box under the counter and pull out a tennis racket.

"Always a wise guy in the bunch."

"You got to pay up before I hand over the key."

"Afraid we'll skip out on you?"

I give him the stink-eye. "Last guest in your room made off with the ashtrays."

"S'alright. None of us smokes anyway." Tooter shells out a five and five ones.

I wait for them to scram before I stash the cash. "A pound of prevention is worth an ounce of cure," Grandma always says.

Hiram the mailman trounces in, plops his heavy leather bag down on the counter, and hands me a handful of letters. "Hey, Sweetheart, got something you've been waiting for."

"A letter from Grandma?"

"Is her name Mildred Donigan?"

My heart does a back flip. After consulting with Dad and Mom, I wrote Grandma and asked her to come live with us. Even though I absolutely love minding the counter—mornings while Mom cleans rooms and Dad fixes leaky faucets, rusty gutters, and broken beds, and afternoons while they launder towels and sheets—I worry what will happen when school starts soon. Not that I'm scared to start a new school. Making new friends should be easy. I hope. It's just that, who'll run the office? How can Dad provide for us without me at the front desk?

* * * * *

"Zowie!" Grandma says in a whistle when she gets off the bus dropping her off in front of us. "This place must've cost you an arm and a leg."

Dad scratches his forehead with his metal claw. "Well, half that, anyway."

Grandma's face turns white, then red. "Lloyd, I . . . uh . . . didn't mean—"

"S'all right, Ma. Any more comments like that, though, and you'll be getting the hook." Dad waves his arm in the air. "You'll be out pounding the streets looking for a new job. And at your age, let me tell you, that won't be a pretty sight."

Grandma's mouth drops open, and for the first time ever, no words come out.

Dad breaks out into a snorting fit. You'd think it's the world-beater of all funnies. Grandma starts giggling and presto, our parking lot is a regular vaudeville auditorium. Even Mom chuckles.

When the hilarity dies down, I grab Grandma by the elbow and chauffeur her to her new employment station. "Anything you want to know, just ask me," I say. "For instance, see this stack of papers? Cut each sheet into three by five pieces. Like these." I take out the box of registration cards. "Everybody who stays here writes his name and address. We keep *every* one. Records are *very* important," I point out.

"Here, under the counter is the radio." I jotted down all the shows, which station number they're on and what days and times. "See, for example, *Fibber McGee and Molly* comes on in a coupla hours. *Adventures of Ozzie and Harriet* airs tomorrow. Groucho Marx is on *You Bet Your Life*. Can't say as I like him, but he might be right up your alley. Anyway, you can listen to anything you want 'til a customer shows his mug around here. Then you gotta turn the volume down.

"Now, if some chowderhead comes in and gives you lip, you don't have to be a sucker and take it. Oh yeah, if old man Snooks from next door tries to put the make on you, make a break for it. Last dame he had, he put six feet under." I pause to take a breath and think of what else I need to give Grandma the low down on.

"Heavens to Betsy, child! Such language." Grandma swings me around to face the mirror on the wall behind the counter. "Whatever happened to my sweet little Maxine?"

I'm glad Grandma can tell that I've matured. I shoot a smile at her and she flashes one back. "That reminds me. I've been saving something for you." I rifle through my treasure chest and haul out the Poli-Grip. "This is for your choppers."

It doesn't take Grandma long to get in the groove, and before I know it junior high school skids around the corner.

First day home from my educational pursuit, I'm starved eight-tenths to death and make a beeline for the kitchen. All right! Grandma's all-time famous Snickerdoodles are cooling on wax paper. Looks like I'm going to get first crack at 'em.

Grandma calls from the office desk. "While you're in there, Maxine, put some water on to boil for tea, will you?"

"You betcha," I yell back. I lug a bottle of milk from the icebox and pour a glass full, then settle down for cookie-eating. Melt-in-the-mouth yummy. I'm on my third one when Mom's cigarette smoke floats in through the open kitchen window. She and Dad must be taking a break out back at the picnic table. Can't quite make out what they're saying, so I scooch my chair closer.

"Lloyd, you proved me wrong," Mom says.

"Proved you wrong? About what?" Dad asks.

"About the move. About buying this place."

"I never set out to prove you wrong, Eloise."

"I know. What I'm trying to say is, *I* was wrong."

I can hear Mom puff her Old Gold. More chalky clouds drift in.

"You said I didn't trust you. You were right. I didn't. But I should have. You've never once let me or Maxine down."

Dad starts to say something, but Mom interrupts. "Let me finish, Lloyd. Before, you never needed me. Except for cooking and cleaning." Mom puffs again. "This motor court is hard work, but for the first time we're building something *together*." Mom sighs. "I'm happy, Lloyd. Really happy."

"Me, too," Dad says with a catch in his voice. "Me, too."

The teakettle whistles and Grandma bellers something.

I dump tea leaves in the kettle, grab a sieve, scoop up a plate of Snickerdoodles and a green cup, plus my glass of milk, and set them on a tray to take to Grandma. "What were you yelling about?"

"I wanted to know what was taking so long in there," Grandma says.

When I straighten up, my eyes lock on the mirror behind her. I imagine my daddy winking at me, along with the swell miracle of happiness that just happened by.

"Some things just take time, Grandma," I say.

"BROOKLYN VS. THE BRONX"

October 1, 1947
Brooklyn, New York

Albert buddies up to me. "Francis," he says, "I know I can never replace your Pop, but I'd consider it an honor if you'd call me Dad." He cocks his finger and knuckles the Stetson off his forehead.

I eyeball his skinny mustache what looks like an eyebrow twitching over his fake smile.

After Pa died in Germany in The War, Ma dubbed *me* man of the house, see. Now Al the Pal waltzes over to Brooklyn from the Bronx expecting to lay hands on the joint. He obviously ain't got much space between his ears. On account I'm only ten shouldn't make no difference, he still shoulda asked my permission to marry Ma. Look, I ain't no chump, he ain't gonna give me the bum's rush.

"Tell you what," Al says, "let's have a man's day out, just you and me."

Sounds like a set up. I ain't buying whatever he's selling.

The bozo tries to smooth down my cowlick, then plants a hand on my shoulder. "I hear you're a Dodger's fan," he says, trying to butter me up.

I flinch his hand off.

He sticks it in his fancy-shmancy pinstriped suit pocket, pulls out a coupla tickets stamped:

1947 World Series
Brooklyn Dodgers vs. New York Yankees
Game 3

My heart about takes a powder, but I ain't giving nothing away. Then the lightbulb clicks. "Whaddya a Bronx Bombers buff? 'Cause if yer just trying to rub it in that the Yanks 'r up two games on us—"

"No," he cuts me off. "I've never really followed the Yankees. Of course if you're not interested, I'll take your Mama." He winks a flirt at her.

Later I corner Ma. "I know ya don't like baseball, so I'll go with Al tomorrow so's to save ya the misery."

Ma's lips curl into a dead-giveaway *whew–thanks*.

Ballpark's only a block from the tenements where me'n Ma live. Still I ain't never been to Ebbets Field. Never missed a game, though. See, Pa'd wiggle the RCA knob just right until the station'd come in clear, then we'd hunker down by the window so's to hear the radio announcer *and* real-live cheering. Past couple seasons been mighty lonely sitting by myself.

I can hardly sleep thinking about actually for once in my life being *inside* all the action. Fly-balls sail around in my head. That's what it's gonna be like, probably as close to heaven as I'm gonna get.

Before I know it, I'm walking through the gate! Sure wish Pa was with me instead of this schmuck. Gust of wind hits my face and causes my eyes to water up. Al gawks at me, then fidgets like he ain't never been in a ballpark and don't know what to do.

"Let's get set down," I tell him.

"This way," he says, detouring me with a grimy hand on my shoulder. I wise up soon as I spot the hawkers. Al thinks he can bribe me.

"What gives? No orange Nesbitt?" I say, reaching for my coney dog piled high with the works.

"Hehn, hehn," Al goes, acting like my ketchup splatter on his cufflinks don't bother him none before he steers me all the way down to front row. First base bag's so close I can spit on it. It don't take no private dick to deduce Al's got connections to finagle *these* seats.

Dodgers take the field. I elbow Al and finger Jackie Robinson. "Betcha ain't never seen number 42 before. My man Jackie can play *any* position, except pitcher or catcher, of course. Batting average is outta the park!" I figure I can learn Al a thing or two since he brung me.

"PUH-LAY BAAALL!" the ump bawls.

Since there ain't no action in the first inning, I fill Al in on a few statistics, things he oughta know. Like this here year's the first ever they let a player come over from the Negro League. Jackie Robinson just goes to prove they shoulda done it a long time ago. Things like that. Al listens up and nods his head like it's on a springcoil, on account he's impressed with my expertise.

"Okay, that's enough yapping," I say to shut him up when we level our barrels at pitcher Newsom in the second.

Blam!

Blam!

Newsom can't deliver the goods, so the Yanks bring in Raschi. Fat lot of good it does. Dodgers put the Yanks on the ropes, see. Our sixth run wheels across the plate, and the crowd's so wild ya can't hardly hear yerself shouting. I nab Al around the neck and reel him in. "I told ya we was gonna beat the Bombers. Whad'd I tell ya? Whad'd I tell ya?"

Al flashes his pearly whites and looks all sappy-eyed.

Next couple innings go tit for tat. No sweat. But then DiMaggio stiffs us a scare in the fifth stroking a two-run homer. Yanks start creeping up on us. End of the sixth it's Yanks seven, Dodgers nine. Come the seventh, some Yank pinch hitter named Yogi Berra, what kinda sorry name is Yogi?, swaggers to the plate like he's gonna hit a home run.

"Fat chance. Ain't no pinch hitter ever swatted a homer in the World Series," I say, filling Al in.

"That a fact?" Al grills me, glancing sideways.

I nod.

CRAACK! Danged if Berra don't slam a home run.

"Things change," I say.

Al digs a fingernail into that crack by his eyetooth to pry something loose, then flaps his lips, "That's what I'm hanging my hat on."

"Well, we're hanging by the skin of our teeth to a one-run lead." I cross my fingers.

In the eighth, I hold my breath. It works. Yanks come up goose eggs. 'Course, so do the Dodgers. If we can just keep the Yanks from scoring in the top half of the ninth. I put a lid on the breath-holding in favor of holding something else for good luck. Only thing near is Al. I grab ahold of him and don't let go for nothing. Can't help but notice he ain't got much padding.

Al starts squirming, probably on account of the butt-busting bleachers.

I get a peep at his watch. "Did ya know in the *whole history* of World Series play, ain't *never* been a nine inning game go this long?" I don't really 'spect him to know.

He shoots me a real 'preciative look probably 'cause I'm taking his mind off his sore behind with all this valuable learnin'.

Dodgers finally put him and the Yanks outta their misery and close the books on the game. Nine to eight. I toss my new Dodgers hat in the air, hooting and hollering. "Didn't I tell ya we was gonna win? Huh, Dad? Didn't I tell ya?"

Thunder all around us finally dies down. Al stands up, rubs his fanny, then feels me out. "So, Francis, did you have a good time today?"

"Baseball don't get no better 'n this. It was swell. Just swell." I drain my third bottle of orange Nesbitt and cram leftover peanuts in my good pocket for Ma. "Now that ya know a little something about baseball, and on account of yer connections, maybe ya can get us tickets for the rest of the Series." I flash a smile just for good measure.

Al slaps me on the shoulder. "Today, Son, history was made."

"Yep." I gotta hand it to Al. He's a real quick study.

"CHIEF LESSON"

December 31, 1947
Birmingham, Alabama

"Ruby, tonight we be celebratin'," my momma said, winding thread around her finger and snapping it off. She slipped a new ruffled dress over my head. "Tomorrow be brand-spankin' New Year. Year you be twelve, near growed up." Momma sighed, swatting my be-hind. "Now, go fetch that writin' pad you get for Christmas."

I twirled past the hall mirror, pausing to admire the reflection. Pink satin on black velvet skin. Smooooth.

Once in my room, I perched on the edge of the bed so as not to wrinkle Momma's masterpiece. I pulled the present from underneath my pillow and flipped open Big Chief's red cover to sand-colored paper with wood flecks splattered between the lines.

"RUBY!" Momma hollered. "What be holdin' you up?"

"This leg and this leg," I said, prancing into the kitchen.

Momma rolled her eyes, snatched Big Chief from me. "Child, this pad be your diary. You learn somethin', you write it here." Momma patted Chief's black headdress. "Someday you flip through this here tablet and say, 'Look how much I learnt startin' in 1948. Why I so smart now.'"

The back door creaked open. Polly poked her nine-year-old linen-white face in. Her momma yelled from the stoop for my momma to come on out. Seemed she couldn't get a sitter, so could Polly stay at our house? Not to sleep. No sir, just to stay a couple hours.

Momma clucked her tongue and shook her head at Polly's momma strutting off down the alley. Then she gave me and Polly one of her honey squeezes. "Time you girls be gettin' ready to bring the New Year in proper in the house of the Lord Almighty."

Polly'd never been to my church, so I let her wear my new dress. Figured I'd have plenty of chances later to show it off myself. We sat way up front. The music started, and we commenced shouting and dancing and praising Jesus. Polly's face glowed. Way different than when she sneaked me into *her* church that morning—before they started and nobody was milling around—and hid me in a coat closet that smelled like furniture polish. What I saw through the crack in the door, mmm-mmm. Heaven have mercy. All her people sang with chains on their hearts, faces all sour like they just took a swig of vinegar. Preacher ranted, "Don't do this. Don't do that," and raved about how they were all going to Hell.

In *my* church Polly cried, not because her cousin Snitch was peeking through the window laughing his fool head off. It was more like joy spilling out of her.

Next day, Polly's momma scrubbed her white skin red for wearing my dress, then told her if she ever darkened the doorstep of my church again she would for sure go to Hell.

First day of 1948, I got my pencil and wrote in Big Chief:

Lesson #1:

White folk have outside freedom but don't know nothing about freedom on the inside.
Nobody gonna take that from me.

"ORPHANAGE"

1948
Philadelphia, Pennsylvania

You and the kids are better off without me.

I reread Daddy's scribbling for the hundredth time. It's still a bald-faced lie, but I keep the note because it's all I have of him.

Mother tries hard. In the morning after she gets William, Clem, Violet and me off to school, she takes Ivy with her on the bus to her maid job. After school, us kids go straight home and wait for them. As soon as they get here, Mother warms up something for us to eat. Usually it's leftovers from the house where she works. We have a routine. I wash dishes. Violet dries. Mother sets up her iron and starts in on the baskets of clothes she takes in from rich people. Even with two jobs, she can't pay all our bills, or put enough food on the table to feed the six of us. Weekend meals are especially skimpy.

This evening she rounds us all up. "Kids," she says, then waits 'til her lip stops quivering. "I can find no other way."

I can feel something bad coming.

"We're going to have to . . . temporarily divide up," she says.

"What do you mean divide up?" William, the oldest of us, asks.

Clem sidesteps up to William. "We ain't too good at arithmetic."

A laugh chokes in Mother's throat, then her eyes water up. "I've found a wonderful farm home for you boys with a friend of your father's." She looks at the floor. "You girls will go to a . . . girls' home of sorts in New Jersey."

I can't believe she is splitting us up. "Why can't we all go live with Aunt Sally in Wisconsin? She's got a big house."

Mother wipes her eyes with her apron. "My sister has worries of her own."

"Then how about Gramma Reynolds?" William asks.

"She hasn't regained any strength since her stroke." Mother twists the hem of her apron into a knot.

William argues that since he's thirteen, he can stay here in Philadelphia and earn money to pay his own way and help out. "Johnny told me yesterday he's quitting his newspaper route. I can do that before my first class. After school, I can run errands for Mr. Hogeland at the grocery store. He even asked me about that this weekend."

"Sweet William," Mother says, "you're much too young to carry this burden."

William throws his shoulders back, probably because he considers himself the man of the house. "We managed when Dad went off to war," he says.

"Yes, well, we received his pay from the army. Now, with another mouth to feed—"

"Ivy don't eat much," William states as fact.

"She really doesn't," Violet chimes in.

Mother smiles. She and William debate back and forth. Finally, Mother agrees.

Clem cries so hard Mother almost lets him stay, too. But he's only ten and nobody's going to hire a ten-year-old. She assures him that Daddy's friend really wants him to come. She goes on and on about how he can milk cows, ride a pony, and feed their chickens, even gather the eggs. "Doesn't that sound fun?" she says more than asks.

This whole situation started when Daddy came home from a prisoner of war camp about three years ago. He claimed he was all messed up, but he looked fine to me. I want him here to put a stop to this mess.

Us girls, Violet who's six, Ivy-two, and me, Rose—I'm eleven—don't know what to say. Ivy doesn't get it, and Violet probably thinks it's for a weekend. Nothing seems real right now.

Mother lines us up and goes down the rank putting her hands on our shoulders or in Ivy's case on her head, and says, "William, Clem, Rose, Violet, Ivy, you are my precious bouquet of flowers."

We're all named after posies. William, after Sweet Williams. Clem is short for Clematis. Us girls are pretty much self-explanatory. Except for Ivy. I've never seen an Ivy blossom, but I probably haven't seen everything yet.

Finally, I can speak. "Who will braid my hair?" No matter how busy Mother is, she always takes time to make sure I either have pigtails or a braided pony tail that goes half-way down my back.

"Rose,"—she says and pauses, stroking my hair—"the first of my brunette beauties, I'm sure the nice nuns will see to your needs."

Nuns? We're not even Catholic.

Clem gets sent off first to New York state. Me, Violet, and Ivy end up across the New Jersey state line in Maple Grove Orphanage.

Maple Grove. Sounds all wonderful, like where tall trees with big leaves reach for blue sky, and songbirds flit from branch to branch. A country place where bunnies romp and chipmunks skitter in green grass so thick Ivy could get lost in it.

Ha!

Mother says she picked Maple Grove because it sounds like a place where her flowers will flourish.

Ha again!

"Rose," Mother says to me right before she leaves us in this garden of paradise, "as soon as I am back on my feet, I'll come for you girls and we'll go get Clem together. In the meantime, I'll write every week. Watch over Violet and Ivy. I'm counting on you."

First she announces she's dividing us up and now she's counting on me. Sounds like a lot of math that doesn't add up—a lot more minuses than pluses. Though, like Clem said, "We're not too good at arithmetic." Well, he said "ain't", but "Ain't fell in a bucket of paint." I don't have a lot left, but I do have good grammar.

* * * * *

We've only been here in the Grove Orphanage for a week. Mother's first letter should come any time. While I wait, it doesn't take long to figure out that if it's just me Mother is counting on to take care of my sisters I could do it. The problem is Sister Mary Martha with a mole sprouting out of her face. It's hard to describe the exact location. It's either under her nose or above her lip, but doesn't favor one direction or the other. It has a hair growing out of a hole in the middle of it and when the Sis—we're not supposed to call her that, so

I won't—when Holy Mole Hole breathes in, The Hair gets sucked up her right nostril. When she gets disgusted, which is most of the time, the blast of nose air blows it down over her lip.

It's hard not to stare at her no matter how repulsive it is.

At supper, all fifty-two of us, who they call orphans, line up on hard benches on both sides of long wooden tables. The Mole sits at the end staring us down. If we can't call the nuns Sis, then they shouldn't call us orphans. Over half of us here still have parents.

For no reason, Holy Mole Hole snorts at my new friend Lottie, who is sitting to the side of her. Lottie drops her hand, and her spoon flips from her soup bowl onto the floor. Mole Hole snorts again and licks Lottie's pea soup off her lip. A glop of green hangs off The Hole's nose hair.

One of the rules here is you can't vomit at the table. They should have told us that up front. My punishment is to clean up my puke. I dry heave until my stomach turns inside out. I get sent to bed without any supper. Fine with me. I'll never eat peas again in my life.

*****

Today after classes I have kitchen duty. I ask if Violet can help me dry dishes. This way we can spend more time together. Ivy doesn't get to join us. The Sisters say she will get in our way. Ivy cries when they unwrap her little arms from my leg. Behind my eyes I cry too. How can I watch over her when they take her away? How do I know what she is doing in that room with the other little kids? For all I know, there's a mean girl there. Otherwise, how did Ivy get those bite marks on her arm?

I want to write Mother and tell her about this. The problem is we are not allowed to take paper from our classroom. Or pencils. I wish Mother would write. I suppose she is too tired to.

* * * * *

I have so much to write to Mother. Though it's probably a good thing I can't. Even if I did have paper, where would I get a stamp? Plus, my letters would make Mother feel worse than she already does. I do not have happy things to write about. For example, I would tell her that nobody here does hair. The nuns have theirs all covered up—probably matted messes under those habits. Mother would be stomping mad and sad to hear that Holy Moly called my long hair vanity and then chopped it off. Now I'm all scraggly and ugly. Crying about something a Sister does to you is against the rules. Too bad. Seems like I learn at least a dozen new rules every day.

I am trying my best to keep The Mole and her Nose Hair away from Violet and Ivy.

* * * * *

We've been in this prison six months. Still not one letter from Mother. This is the hardest thing I've ever done in my whole life.

"Don't do this." "Don't do that." "Do it this way, not that way." Holy Mole Hole must not have enough to do because she goes around making up stuff that's forbidden. For instance, at bedtime she comes to our dormitory with a ruler and measures the window shades. We're supposed to pull them down to exactly twelve inches above the windowsill. First off, none of us—now fifty-eight inmates—has a ruler. Second off, the shades are on a sprung spring roller. When you pull it down, or up, doesn't matter, it goes S-P-R-O-I-N-G. Flap, flap, flap, and ends up where it wants. Sometimes it's halfway to the floor. Other times, it winds up tight, clear at the top. We have to scoot one of our beds over and coax it down while tottering on our tiptoes on the skinny headboard.

Why do they call it a head*board* when it's made out of iron? Because when your head hits it your brains turn to sawdust?

Speaking of trees, if only we had landscape pictures—or pictures of any kind—on our dormitory walls it wouldn't feel so bleak here. At least my bedroom at home had a fake painting of a mountain and waterfall. Sometimes I would imagine myself standing in the scene. Here, there is nothing to escape to.

I miss my mother something awful. Violet sticks to me like paste, but only when Holy Mole Hole isn't around. There's a rule about sticking to somebody like paste. Ivy cries a lot. I rock her every chance I get. We sneak into the toilet together so I can hold her. There's a rule against rocking kids, too.

But Mother's counting on me.

I go into the Head Sister's office when nobody's looking and steal some paper and a pencil. Since grammar is my specialty, I just as well put it to good use. I write a letter expressing my views on a few things. Like the holier-than-thou attitude around here. And how it isn't right-eous for them to make us work like slaves, scrubbing cold, hard stone steps on our bony knees with our pruned-up fingers in icy buckets of water. I ask if they are trying to show us what Hell is like. Not that I expect an answer, of course. I write a whole lot more but most of it isn't repeatable.

I don't show it to anybody. I'm sure there are rules against that—writing and showing. I hide the letter under my pillow. Guess there are rules against that, too, because somehow Holy Mole ends up with it in her grubby hands. I'm pretty sure none of the other girls had anything to do with the discovery. Even though I didn't sign it, it's obvious where it came from, being under my pillow and all.

Mother Maria Agnes, the nun at the top—who William would call the Big Dog—calls me into her office. Holy Mole Hole is there with her arms crossed and a smirk on her face. I could kiss Mother Maria Agnes when she tells The Mole she can leave the room. I've never seen anyone kiss a nun, but probably because there are rules against that.

"Did you write this?" Mother Maria Agnes asks about my letter in her hand.

I know for sure there are rules against lying, so I weigh my options. Which will get me in the most trouble? I tell the truth, hoping the message of what I wrote will get across to her.

Our talk lasts about half-an-hour. Mother Maria Agnes thanks me for being honest.

When I open the door to leave, The Mole tumbles in and falls down. I'm pretty sure there shouldn't be any rules against me opening the door. It isn't my fault she was pressing on it.

Nothing changes as a result of my letter. Other than Holy Mole watches me like a hawk now.

Something does happen, though. Little four-year-old Emily was here when I came, and now she's not. Word in the halls is she died from appendicitis. In my opinion, she died from a broken heart. At her memorial service, a new nun, Sister Angelica, talks about how happy Emily is now that she is in the arms of Jesus. I am glad for Emily.

I am angry at Mother for bringing us here and for counting on me, especially since we haven't had even one word from her since she went out those gates. I am mad at Daddy for abandoning us. A part of me wants to get mad at Ivy for being a clinging vine. But it isn't her fault. Now I feel guilty for even thinking that. I love Ivy and Violet. They're all I have left.

Except guilt. Mole Hole does a pretty good job of drilling that into us.

* * * * *

Tonight The Mole barrels up and down the aisle between the ends of our beds, as usual. We all quit breathing for fear we are doing something that will get us in trouble. Finally, she leaves. Tonight we are all lucky. Our regular breathing doesn't start up, though, until we hear her in the room below us. We wait for her snores to rattle up through the wall vents into our dormitory.

We cross our fingers that Sister Angelica will wait for The Mole's snores before coming to pray and tuck us in. Tonight Sister Angelica shows up before any snoring starts up. Uh-oh. You can hear a pin drop. Not that any of us have a pin. There's a rule against having pins.

Sister Angelica is so sweet, we don't even need sugar on our porridge when she sits at the breakfast bench-table with us. Not that they serve sugar in the first place. Sweet Sister told us there's a shortage of sugar here, even though the war is over. I asked Sweet Sister if that's the case, why are we prisoners? Her laugh sounds like music, but not like the chants they make us sit through in the sanctuary.

Since right about the time I wrote that note, Sweet Sister's been coming every night. It is the highlight of our days.

We hear footsteps.

"What are you doing here?" Holy Mole Hole demands of Sweet Sister.

"I have come to pray with the girls and tuck them in," Sweet Sister says softly.

"That is against the rules!" Holy Mole Hole growls.

Sweet Sister smiles.

"We'll see what Mother Superior has to say about insubordination," Holy Hole hisses.

Sweet Sister stands her ground and kindly gives The Mole a little lesson from the Bible about love and mercy.

All the air sucks out of the room. Nobody can breathe.

In the morning, Mother Maria Agnes calls us all to assembly. Lottie whispers, "We're all in for it now." There's a rule that if one of us sins then all must repent and face the consequences. That's because when one of us is out of whack the rest are affected. That's the logic they use around here.

Lottie's knees start to shake so bad she can hardly walk. Violet and Ivy cling to my skirt. My legs wobble.

Ivy starts to cry for Mother. She swipes her snot and tears on my sleeve—right where a hole is. My skin slimes up.

I hate it more than ever that Mother is counting on me. I'm going to steal some more paper—I still have the pencil under the foot of my mattress. I'll write Mother a letter to let her know she can just start counting on somebody else because there's nothing I can do about anything here. Maybe I can give it to Sweet Sister to mail.

After Mother Marie Agnes's sermon on Godliness, Sweet Sister leads me into the little chapel off the sanctuary. It is peaceful in here with candlelight dancing on the dark wooden walls and high ceiling. Jesus is hanging on the cross behind the altar. That's another thing that isn't right. According to the

Bible they took Him down and put Him in the tomb. Then He left there and flew up to heaven.

Sweet Sister motions me to the front pew to sit beside her. She pulls me close and smooths my short, tangled hair, then kisses the top of my head. She smells good. Clean, like Mother's Ivory soap.

My heart beats a hundred miles an hour. I can't stop my tears.

Sweet Sister holds me for a long time. Finally, she says, "Rose, when I was younger, I dreamed of having a daughter like you."

"No you didn't," I say.

"Why do you say that?" She lifts my chin in her hand.

"Nobody wants me. Not my daddy. Not my mother. Nobody." I start to cry again.

Sweet Sister pulls something out of the folds of her robe and places a bundle in my hands.

I can't believe what I'm seeing. A whole packet of envelopes addressed to me in Mother's handwriting.

"It is against the rules for children to receive letters from their parents. When it was allowed, children would withdraw and cry for days. We don't want to cause any of you even greater homesickness. The plan is to give you these upon your departure." She sounds sad. "I've been in much prayer over this, and even though I am breaking the rules, I believe this is what God wants me to do."

My tongue is swollen in my mouth and my heart feels like it's going to thump out of my body.

Sweet Sister goes on, "At the beginning, your mother wrote you once a week. Now her letters come once a month. Still, she is faithful."

"She didn't forget us?" I whisper.

"No, she did not." Sweet Sister folds her hands over mine. "Rose, when you first came, you were such a sweet child. It breaks *my* heart to see *your* heart become hardened." She pauses and takes a deep breath. "Last night, after Sister Mary Martha left, you said some awful things about her."

"Well, she makes me so mad I just want to punch her in her hairy mole hole!"

Sweet Sister presses a finger to her lips. She raises her eyes to the ceiling. At last she says, "Anger is a prison of your own making, Rose." Sweet Sister cradles my face in her hands so I'm looking her in the eyes. "Some people go through life bitter and resentful over what they're dealt . . . whether it be their looks, being orphaned, financial ruin, having unspeakable things done to them as a child—" Sweet Sister's voice catches, and her eyes close. It looks like she's trying to snuff out whatever it is she sees behind her eyelids. She stays that way so long it starts to scare me. I clear my throat and wiggle in the pew. Sweet Sister opens her eyes and looks at Jesus on the cross.

"You know He is not still there, don't you?" she asks, but doesn't wait for an answer. "The cross is really empty." She looks at me. "Jesus is in here." Sweet Sister pats her heart. "That is why I have no room for anger."

I'm glad Sweet Sister agrees with me that they shouldn't have Jesus still hanging up there.

"Rose, Sister Mary Martha needs your love more than she knows. She is more to be pitied than censored," Sweet Sister says.

Even though grammar is my specialty, I'm not exactly clear on this censored thing. I'll look it up later.

A smile twitches at the corner of Sweet Sister's mouth, then she gets serious. "You really should not use Holy in the same sentence as Mole Hole. It is sacrilege."

In all the times that Sister Mary Martha tried to shame me, it never came close to the shame I feel right now. My heart splits in two at my double whammy of doing God wrong and disappointing Sister Angelica.

Sweet Sister goes on, "Something I have come to realize is that anger has its roots in feeling helpless. There are lots of things in life over which we have no control. However, you do have a choice as to whether you want to be angry or want to love.

"I love you, Rose," she says. "I hope and pray you will be able to love Sister Mary Martha in spite of her being so hard on you girls. If you get this lesson right, the rest of life will come much easier for you." She presses my fingers to her lips then places them gently in my lap. "Now, scoot. Go read your mother's letters to Violet and Ivy."

I skip down the aisle.

"Oh, and, Rose."

My heart skips a beat. Did she change her mind?

"I will need the letters back right away. I do not want to be the cause of any trouble for you and your sisters."

I find Violet coming out of her classroom. I grab her hand and practically run to the nursery for Ivy. I tell the nun there that Sister Angelica has told me to come get Ivy, so she lets her go. On the way to the bathroom I snag Lottie and ask her to be a lookout because the restroom door doesn't lock. I breathe a sigh of relief when there isn't anybody else in here.

Violet's eyes go wide when she sees our treasure. Even though I have to hurry and give them back to Sister Angelica, I don't want to miss a single word.

Mother has been so busy. She and William are working their guts out. Her letters are full of hope.

I hear Lottie say on the other side of the door, "Dear Sister Mary Margaret, how are you this fine day?"

Quickly, I plop Ivy on the toilet and send Violet to the next stall before I stash the letters in the trash and cover them up with garbage.

The Mole barges in. "What are you up to?"

"Sister Angelica sent me to get Ivy. Seems she's got a bit of the trots."

Is a half a lie as bad as a whole one?

* * * * *

Sweet Sister's lesson is hard to do. I am practicing on loving Mole Hole. I start by not staring at her mole, or the hair in the hole. I try to look in her eyes and smile. It shocked her the first time I did.

My next step is to call her by her real name, Sister Mary Martha. Jesus' mother's name was Mary, so maybe if I think of that when I look at Sister, it will help me stay on the right path.

Tomorrow I am going to try to hug Sister Mary Martha with my eyes. There shouldn't be a rule against that.

* * * * *

It's been five hundred twenty-six days and four hours that we've been in Maple Grove Orphanage.

Sweet Sister comes running into our classroom. There's a rule against running, but she looks excited about something. "Rose, your mother is here!" she shouts. There's a rule about shouting, too.

Mother and William, who looks like a young man now, have come to fetch us girls. Mother is all tears and smiles and hugs. William keeps clearing his throat.

Mother announces, "I got a position as a governess with the Sinclairs in upstate New York. He's some hotshot lawyer and she's an heiress of a big industrialist. They've got a cottage behind their mansion. It's small, but certainly more than what we're accustomed to."

My heart thrums in my ears. Did I hear right?

"They have a girl, Constance, who is Violet's age. The Mrs. is hopeful you girls will be good companions for her. She has been tutored at home since the automobile accident that paralyzed her legs, so has been without friends on a daily basis for almost two years now. The Mrs. also said William and Clem can assist the gardener after school."

Is this too much to hope for?

"I'll be back in a flash," I say, and run (What're they going to do to me for running now?) to find Sweet Sister—who disappeared around the corner down the hall—to thank her for her prayers.

I don't have to go far to find her. Here she comes with Sister Mary Margaret. I throw my arms around Sweet Sister and thank her. She hugs me tight. When she lets go, Sister Mary Margaret sidles up to me. Her hand kind of touches mine. I look up at her but her eyes are straight ahead. I put an arm around her waist and squeeze. Only not so hard as to cause that tear to come to her eye.

Mother comes near us holding Ivy in her right arm and clenching Violet's palm with her free hand. "It looks as if you made some friends here," she says, then does a double take as if she hasn't really looked me over since she got here. "What in the world happened to your hair?"

I feel Sister Mary Margaret stiffen.

Everything goes quiet. Even Sweet Sister holds her breath. Mother lets go of Violet's hand and runs her fingers through what hair I have left. I can see her jaw tighten as she looks from one Sister to the other.

"It'll grow back," I say and turn toward the door. "Let's go get Clem. He's counting on us."

"CRIPPLER"

August, 1949
Ogallala, Nebraska

Rubbing her neck, Nora thought of her cousin Suzie who'd complained of a stiff neck at the end of the school year.

"That's how it started," Suzie had said. Now she lay partially paralyzed. The doctors gave her no hope of ever walking again.

Nora broke out in a sweat—not because of the heavy bushel basket of wet clothes she lugged to the clothesline under the summer sun—but because of old lady Beezle. Nora's neck became rigid at the mental mention of her name. *Still,* Nora scolded herself, *I ought to be thankful she gave me the job in the first place.*

She swelled with pride at landing the soda jerk job, coveted by all the town girls, at Beezle's Pharmacy. Living a mile outside of Ogallala near the Platte River, Nora wasn't considered a *town* girl. Some of her freshman classmates—Bonnie Busbaum and Mavis Kruckshank, to name a couple—had stopped talking to her, obviously envious of her position in the limelight. The drugstore, nicknamed by high-schoolers as *The Watering Hole*, served as *the* meeting place for teens since the shop's soda fountain offered the best chocolate malted milkshakes and lemon-lime-vanilla phosphates in the county.

Even though she'd been on the job a couple of months, yesterday she'd made a sickening mistake. At the mere thought of it, Nora's stomach churned. Instead of reaching for whole milk, she'd grabbed buttermilk to make a shake for the Baptist preacher's wife. Oh, the Christian lady was nice enough about it, but old lady Beezle had a cow. She also had a policy. One she enforced without exception, "You make a mistake, you drink it. All of it."

Nora shuddered at the still-sour taste.

"You kids stay out of the canal!"

Mom's voice rescued Nora from her preoccupation with the debacle.

"Did you hear me?" Mom called to Nora's brothers as they headed down the path toward Drummy's pond. Mike carried the fishing poles in one hand and a can of dirt with worms in the other. Nora knew Mike didn't trust Donny, only five, with such valuables.

Nora also knew why the worry in her Mom's voice. A kid in Nora's class had gone swimming in a canal, runoff from the Platte, three weeks ago and days later came down with Polio. Infantile Paralysis the *Rockford Chronicle* called it. Her cousin and this classmate weren't the only ones in town who'd gotten it, either. Jed Donovan, the first to come down with it, had died. Kids all over the United States were dropping like hackberry pods.

Fear was as contagious as the paralyzing epidemic.

Attempting to shake off the possibility of it, Nora recalled remedies people resorted to, to beat the attacker. Old Indian arrow poison. DDT sprayed over Ogallala from an airplane. Obviously the spray hadn't killed the culprit in the canal's infected water.

Nora swatted away a fly buzzing her face as she hooked the clothespin bag over the line's taut wire. Soon the clothesline would sag from sopping clothes fresh squeezed through the wringer washer. From the back porch, the choppy rhythm of the machine agitating the next load reminded her she mustn't dally. The fly, joined by a comrade, persisted in swarming around her head.

Virus in fly-contaminated food. Thoughts from an article identifying the source of Polio hummed through her mind. The droning of it sent shivers down her spine.

Determined not to let dread spoil this glorious day, she drew a breath of fresh, earthy air from the just-over summer shower. Closing her eyes, she tilted back her head and massaged the hardness settling in her neck. She lingered in the sun's warmth, letting it bathe her soul and spirit. As the rays washed over her, she smiled.

Nora delighted in helping her mom more on Mondays than any other day. It gave her a sense of purpose, a sense of usefulness. It was what being a woman was all about. Well, she wasn't quite a woman—yet. As a matter of fact, it would be a few years before she would be considered one. Even though she had started her "period" four months ago. That's why it was important to her to get the proper training to become a housewife, especially if her soda jerk career didn't pan out.

Today she and her mom washed clothes. Tomorrow they would sprinkle them, roll them up tight, then tuck the cloth fists snugly into the bushel basket to moisten properly. Wednesday meant ironing. Thursday normally brought baking, but since it was August, this week Thursday and Friday she and Mom would can the second crop of beans, corn, and a batch of tomatoes and tomato juice. The thought of drawing a long draught of hot tomato juice triggered her salivary glands.

As Nora swallowed at the expectation, her stomach flip-flopped. She dismissed the nausea as hunger pangs. Or maybe it was that horrible buttermilk shake catching up with her.

Drawing a pillowcase from the basket at her feet, she bracketed her thumbs inside the rectangular case and shook it out before pinning it to the line. A breeze immediately filled the big pocket and lifted it like a windsock.

I'd love to fly. Again, she closed her eyes and tilted her face skyward. *Ah, the freedom of it.* She allowed herself to soar, just as she did when bicycling down Smithy's Hill. She loved the feel of wind against her face and the unrestrained movement it brought. Her mom had admonished her time and again of how unladylike it was for her to bicycle in a dress. Nora didn't care. The catching of the wind in her skirt gave her the sense of sailing. Not that she'd ever been on a boat. But someday she would add that to her experiences. She imagined herself hoisting the sail and jibbing the jibe, or whatever it was that sailors did.

"Nora!"

The call of her name snatched Nora back to land. *Guess the closest I'll ever come to flying is down Smithy's Hill.*

"Land sakes, girl. Daydreaming again? I've got another basket of clothes ready to hang, and here you've only fastened one pillowcase. At this rate it'll take us a month of Sundays to get done." Nora's mom stood with her hands on her hips, her flour-sack apron snapping in the breeze.

"Mondays," Nora said.

Mom's sparse eyebrows pinched together in a question.

"A month of Mondays. Not a month of Sundays." Nora giggled.

Mom's mouth twitched. A chuckle seeped from her throat. Then she bubbled from the belly up. Nora loved making her mom laugh, loved watching crow's feet skitter out the corners of her eyes.

Mom's laughter stuttered to a stop. Curvy lines crawled across her forehead. "You look hot, Nora." Mom neared and palmed her face. "Feels like you've got a fever."

"Probably just been in the sun too long." Nora swept her mom's hand away. "I'm thirsty." Nora headed for the kitchen, letting the rickety, wooden screen door slam behind her. At the sink, she turned on the cold water and filled a glass—a promotional gift inside a box of laundry detergent. She drank. The coolness felt good against the heat of her throat. Not soothing, though. It hurt to swallow. She traipsed back outside to finish hanging laundry.

By the middle of the afternoon Nora had a raging headache—something she rarely, if ever, got. At five o-clock, taking down the last of the stiff, dry blue jeans and stacking them in the basket, she could hardly raise her arms. Her muscles felt rigid. Her stomach roiled. She could barely swallow for the scratchiness in her throat. Her legs threatened to fail.

All night long, she wretched into a waste can beside her bed. Her fever mounted. Consumed with vomiting, she experienced horrendous back and spinal pain. Her right arm metamorphosed into a lead weight. Then her left arm. Unbelievable leg pain signaled immobility. By the end of the week, all four of her limbs proved useless and nothing more than dead wood.

She only gained comfort from her mother's ever-present and ever-soothing cool rag across her forehead. But that meant her mother was ignoring the garden and canning. Nora felt bad that she was taking such valuable time away from duties needing to be done.

On the advice of her doctor, her parents kept her isolated at home until the fever broke and she would no longer be contagious. Her brothers slept in the barn and weren't allowed to come into the house even to eat.

As the second week drew to a close, Nora's temperature finally dipped below 101 degrees.

*****

Nora awoke. *Where am I?* Her nose itched. She tried to raise a hand to scratch it. Nothing happened. She looked around. In a bed not her own and unable to turn her head, glancing askance, she searched for answers. A white curtain surrounded her bed. Voices came from the other side.

"Mrs. Parrish, even though you did take Nora to the dentist to fill her teeth, there's still no evidence that's how she contracted Polio."

"But, Doctor, I read in *Time* magazine that a dentist and a bacteriologist were sure that's how the disease is spread."

"Conjecture. Purely conjecture. There are theories that it's spread through raw milk or by rats, too." Nora heard the doctor sigh before continuing. "But the long and short of it is . . . we simply don't know."

Nora's mom burst into sobs.

Fear seized Nora. Her insides felt paralyzed too.

*****

When she awoke again, it took her a second to remember where she was, and why she was there. It took but a moment to recall the grief in her mom's voice, in her tears. Nora steeled herself. She willed herself to not make this any more difficult on her mom than it already was. She would do whatever it took to walk again.

A chubby nurse in a starched uniform and crisp white hat pulled back the curtain. "Good morning, Nora. My name is Stella." She smiled with bright red lips and green eyes. "We're going to be spending a lot of time together, which I hear from your mom, is not such a bad deal for me." She winked. "I understand you've got a good sense of humor and that you are a hard worker."

Nora started to nod her head, but even that felt like a board.

"See, already you're trying to make those rebellious muscles get to work. Good job. Take it slow. We'll start with your fingers. One step at a time. Well, not exactly a step. Your legs are the last things we'll tackle." Stella's fleshy cheeks turned even pinker. "Oh dear, I don't mean to say we'll actually tackle—"

"Well, if you do, you'll probably come out on top because I doubt I'll get very far," Nora said. The image of the rather plump Stella wrestling her to the floor made her smile. But the vision of herself not being able to move at all triggered tears.

Stella's gentle hand comforted as it wiped moisture from Nora's cheeks. At the same time, this simple act of kindness pointed out Nora's inability to attend to even the most basic of routines.

Before coming here, Mom had fed her, or at least tried to spoon broth past her lips. Mom had turned her in bed. But the most debilitating function—or dysfunction—proved to be urinating and bowel movements. Both unyielding tasks. Nora hated burdening her mom. Now she would have to rely on strangers for everything. Overwhelmed with despair, Nora spiraled into the darkness of depression. She wanted to die.

She closed her eyes in the wishing of it. *At least those muscles aren't frozen.* That bit of good news flickered then faded out of the grasp of her normally ever-present friends—Humor and Hope.

For the next several days, Nora fought. Fought against tears. Fought to open her eyes to reality. Fought to breathe, for each breath brought one more moment of immobility. The battle sapped what motes of strength she had left. In spite of all her efforts toward movement, results didn't so much as rise over the rails of her bed. The embarrassment of catheters and enemas demolished every last ounce of self-respect.

From the bed beyond the curtain, Nora heard a whimper. Surprised to have a roommate, she envisioned a girl of fourteen lying as straight as Beezle's soda countertop. The image repulsed, then saddened her. *Am I only imagining myself?*

Stella bounced into the room. "How's my girl today?" Her smile pierced a tiny hole in Nora's darkness. Sliding the curtain on its track to the side, Stella announced, "Today, you have two firsts. Meet Lila. She just moved in here from down the hall."

Nora shifted her eyes as far as they could go to the left. "Hi, Lila."

The girl had her eyes closed and didn't respond.

"Well, she's asleep. You'll get to know each other in good time." Stella winked.

"What's the other first?"

"Today, Sunshine, we start therapy."

Sunshine. Even though Nora felt far from sunny, and didn't feel too bright for that matter, she liked that Stella called her that.

"We should have begun this before now but your fever spiked. The doctor wanted to make sure you were stabilized before we put any more stress on your body." Stella folded back

Nora's sheet and blanket. "The sooner we put your muscles in motion, the better chance you have at regaining movement."

After firmly massaging Nora's arms and legs, Stella sent for an orderly to help move Nora to a whirlpool bath. As they lifted her from bed, Nora realized the truth of the mental image she'd had of herself. Indeed, she was a plank. Stella carried her by her feet, the orderly with his hands locked under her armpits. When they reached the therapy room, they slowly lowered her into a butterfly-shaped tank. At first frightened of sinking like a rock and drowning, Nora relaxed—if only internally—upon learning of the support beneath her body.

Stella winked. "Okay, Sunshine, no more lounging around." She turned to the therapists. "I hear she's a hard worker. Prove her mother right." With that Nora's favorite nurse disappeared into the hallway.

The therapists swept Nora's arms and legs out and back, to the side in arches and back again. Nora imagined herself making snow angels. In that instant, she realized Polio did not control her completely. What had often plagued Mom about her would be just the thing to save her—daydreaming, woolgathering. Mom could name it whatever she wanted, but Nora decided to call it her "Wings."

I may never fly in a plane, but Wings will lift me up.

Glad for all the practice she'd had in this mental art, for the first time in weeks Nora allowed herself the prospect of conquering paralysis. Even now, she imagined the wind in her face as she flew down Smithy's Hill on the wheels of memories. Before she knew it, she was back in her room with steam packs on her arms and legs.

Working her over, Stella lectured, "We've got to get messages from your brain to your motor nerves. Right now your muscles aren't receiving these cues. Danger lies in muscles atrophying and clinging to what good muscles you do have. If that happens, they'll lock up as well." Removing the wet packs, Stella drew a deep breath. "Okay, we're going to s-t-r-e-t-c-h. Are you ready?"

"Let me warm up with a couple of calisthenics first."

"Well, aren't you just the comical one?" Stella chuckled.

Nora liked that she could make Stella laugh. Two things she could do already. Hope poked its head over the horizon.

Stella slipped her hands under Nora's ankles and slowly pulled upward.

Pain shot through Nora's body. She clenched her teeth, determined not to complain, even if Hope had taken a dive. Stella continued to lift. Finally, the torment too much, Nora screamed.

"Just a little more, Kiddo. We need to separate atrophied muscles from active ones." Stella held her breath then let out air in one long whoosh. "Little by little, we'll increase your range of motion."

Nora couldn't stop her tears from escaping. If only she could clench her fists, grab onto something to stem the tide of this torture. The last few inches Stella raised her legs, almost sent Nora into unconsciousness. Almost. She was catapulted back into the here and now by Stella's pronouncement.

"Eventually, Kiddo, we'll pull your legs back over your head."

"Great. And I didn't think I had anything to look forward to."

Stella burst out laughing. "Your mother warned me about your sense of humor at the most unsuspecting times."

Mom. Nora needed her more than ever. But, she knew, the hour-plus drive from the farm to the North Platte Hospital was more than Mom could manage, both financially and time-wise. She didn't expect Dad to break away from his tractor to come. Still, she wished Mom were here despite the improbability.

Mom had stayed faithfully by Nora's side during her first two weeks of hospitalization. She sighed at repercussions they would all face this winter. There would not be enough canned vegetables, for they had missed the second crop of beans and corn. Unless neighbors had come to harvest the tomatoes, there would be no juice for drinking, or for chili.

I am nothing but a burden.

Upon departure yesterday, Mom promised, "I'll come as often as I can."

Nora knew that likely meant every Sunday at the most and had insisted a letter would be good enough. If Mom would give Nora's friends Jean and Patsy the hospital's address, that would be plenty. Besides, Nora didn't want people staring at her, even Mom, in this helpless state. That would only serve as a reminder of the burden she was. As soon as she could move, she would welcome visitors.

Plus, mail would give Nora something to look forward to.

* * * * *

The day after Lila moved in, Stella drew back the curtain separating the beds and left it that way upon exiting their room. Especially glad that Stella had positioned her on her side facing her roommate, Nora studied the tiny girl with short-cropped hair. *Peter Pan*, Nora thought. Lila, also lying on her side, opened her eyelids. Nora had never seen such big brown eyes—outside of her calf, Elsie.

"Hi, I'm Nora. I'd hop over and shake your hand but I'm kind of indisposed at the moment." She grinned. "That makes two."

Lila's eyes questioned.

"Two exterior body muscles that actually work," Nora explained. "Eyelids and mouth."

Lila laughed. "I'm Lila."

If Nora could have jumped back, she would've. Lila's voice, just a shade shy of booming, sent Nora into chuckles and snorts.

"What's so funny?" The rumble of words from such a tiny body shoved silence out the door, making way for Nora's laughter.

Tears streamed down the side of Nora's face and melted into the pillow. Finally, able to speak, she said, "Your voice doesn't match your size."

Lila sighed. "When I was little, I drank something I shouldn't have. They still don't know if it was acid or what. It affected my vocal chords."

Shame rushed over Nora. "I . . . I'm sorry."

"Don't be."

A ruckus echoed in the hallway just outside their door. A second later, a tall boy busted into the room toting a large poster. Behind the "Get well, Froggy. We miss you." giant card, Bonnie Busbaum flipped her ponytail off her shoulder. Spying Nora, she sprinted to her bed. "Nora, I'm soooo sorry you got Polio. But don't worry about your job at Beezle's. I'm taking your place since you won't be back. I know you wanted to try out for cheerleader, but you wouldn't want to be one anyway 'cause Jean and Patsy won the tryouts, and who wants to be associated with them? Blah, blah, blah . . . ."

Jean and Patsy are cheerleaders? Why didn't they tell me?

"Hey, Bonnie, put a lid on it. She don't want to hear all that." The boy stepped beside Bonnie and tugged at her arm.

Bonnie flinched away from his grip. "If I were laying here all incapacitated and missing out on everything, I'd sure want to know what's going on." She planted a hand on her waist in a *so-there.*

Although Bonnie's lips continued to flap, Nora disconnected from the sound. More profoundly, she was disconnected from her job, from school, from her friends. From living. The disconnection suddenly sucked every bit of air from the room. Walls closed in on her. A coffin of confinement pronounced death. Death of life as she had known it.

"Nora." The gravelly voice punched a hole in the descending darkness.

Nora realized Lila was talking.

"This is my brother, Dave." Lila swept her gaze toward the handsome boy at the end of her bed.

Dave stepped toward Nora and held out his hand. "Pleased to meet ya." Immediately, his face flushed the color of a ripe tomato. He swung his palm to his head and nonchalantly combed fingers through his hair.

Nora forced away images of Jean and Patsy leaping in the air, cheering on the basketball team. "I'm . . . I'm not quite used to this paralysis thing myself."

Laughing nervously, Dave turned to Lila. "Well, Sis, I gotta go."

Dave and Bonnie's exit drained something from the room. To Nora, it felt like somebody had pulled the plug on pretending.

Lila started to cry.

Nora wanted to as well. *Why not? I don't have anything else to do.* She slowly forced her head away from Lila. After several minutes of sobbing, Nora decided all crying did was fill her ears with tears—a pool different than that which had formed during her laugh at Lila's voice. This time Nora minded that she couldn't dab the puddle away. At last to shatter the stillness, she said, "Your brother is nice."

"He's okay. More a goofball than anything."

"How old is he?" Nora glanced sideways.

"Sixteen." Lila's calf eyes shone with pride.

Nora wondered if Lila was as young as she looked. "How old are you?"

"Twelve. How old are you?"

"Fourteen. How did Bonnie meet Dave?" Nora couldn't imagine what Dave saw in Bonnie or what kind of circumstances might have brought them together.

"Her grandparents live next door."

"Next door where? I mean where are you from?"

"Oshkosh."

Stella breezed into the room. "Time for calisthenics, girls."

* * * * *

Whirlpool baths, steam packs, massages, and excruciating stretching exercises sandwiched between lying around and more lying around, extended into two long months for Nora and Lila, the monotonous routine broken only by family visits. Nora's Mom, Dad, and brothers came on Sunday after church and Lila's parents popped in every Saturday, Dave on Wednesdays.

Yay! Today's Wednesday. Nora found herself looking forward to Dave's mid-week drop by after school. He talked with her like she was normal. Her own brother, Donny, did too. But Mike acted like he couldn't stand to be around her. She figured her parents made him come anyway. Dad fidgeted a lot and looked sad every time he looked at her.

Pity accompanied those who passed through the door, visiting more often than any one person. Embarrassment also showed up quite regularly.

Jean and Patsy had come only once. Although they'd sent a card or two, they kept their messages short, and it seemed to Nora, dutiful.

Maybe after I get home things will return to normal. Or as normal as a wheelchair will allow. The wheelchair wouldn't be forever; of that Nora was certain.

Dave trooped into the room. "Hey, Lila. Hey, Nora." His eyes twinkled in mischief.

Lila eyed her brother. "You're up to something."

"You guys want to play a joke on Stella?" He reached into his letterman's jacket and pulled out a Mason jar filled with gold liquid and didn't wait for the girls' consent before heading for Lila's plastic urine bag hanging beside her bed. Lila had had a setback and had reverted to the catheter.

Nora felt sorry for her but was glad for her own bedpan progress, even though it meant being lifted and set onto the cold metal and being bent into a lazy "L" by two nurses.

Carefully disconnecting the bag, Dave drained it into the sink then filled it with the jar's contents. No sooner had he hooked it back up than Stella sailed into the room. "Hi, Dave. Glad you could make it. The girls so look forward to your visits." She strode to Lila's bed and glanced at the urine bag. "Looks like you're drinking enough liquids." With efficiency, she charted the amount of fluid then unclipped the bag. In three steps she was at the sink emptying it. Immediately, she jumped back. "Merciful Mother of Mysteries!"

"What in the . . . ?"

Even from her bed, Nora detected the heady odor of apple cider vinegar.

Stella fixed a glare on Lila, then on Dave.

Dave burst into guffaws. Lila joined in, her bass voice croaking like a frog. Nora laughed so hard her insides felt like jiggling jelly. Stella's chagrin contorted into confusion, then cartwheeled into the fun of it.

"Mister Smarty Pants, you're going to be the death of me." Stella turned the faucet on full blast.

After she left, Dave strolled to the space between their beds. "I've been thinking." His face took on a serious note. He placed his hands flat against his legs. "What if your index fingers and thumbs could spider crawl?" He demonstrated a finger-over-thumb climb up his leg onto his stomach, chest, neck, and onto his face. "See . . . that way you could scratch your nose when it itches."

Having regained partial use of her fingers although not yet her hands or arms, Nora brightened. Slowly, she leapfrogged her right index finger over her thumb and began the ascent up her body. As she rested her palm on her hip, the weight of her hand pulled it off to the side, depositing it onto the mattress. Waiting but a moment to regain strength, she resumed the strain of engaging the few muscles that did work. Pushing past discomfort, she exerted every iota of energy she could muster. Sweat beaded on her lip. She refused to blow it away. This time she would flick it off with her finger. Minutes later, her hand finally rested across her mouth!

"Stella," she shouted. "Stella, come here!"

From the hallway, Nora heard a cart crash against the wall, followed by a scurrying of feet. Stella burst into the room, fear flashing in her eyes.

Already, Nora's fingers were on the move, creeping along her cheek, over her eyebrow, and veering toward the top of her head. The journey culminated in a one-finger scratch.

Stella and Dave clapped, cheered, and hugged. A less mild version of the applause erupted over a raspy "Hurray!" from Lila's bed. Nora joined in the jubilation at Lila's own little miracle—the crook of her arm embracing her head against the pillow.

Rushing to the hallway, Stella hailed doctors and nurses to share in the marvel. People packed the room in pandemonium. Since her arrival, Nora had not experienced this much excitement, this much hope for normalcy.

When all but Stella and Dave had gone, Nora motioned her nurse close with an index finger. "Stella, you said we were going to take this one step at a time. Turns out you were right. Finger steps. Who would've guessed?" She opened her palm for Stella's embrace and squeezed the nurse's warm hand clutching hers.

Singing *Itsy Bitsy Spider went up the water spout*, Stella practically skipped out the door.

Nora shot a thumbs-up to Lila. "We're getting there, Lila. We'll be walking before you know it."

Lila smiled faintly. "You will walk again, Nora."

"You too."

"I don't think so."

The tone of Lila's words scared Nora. "Don't talk like that. Sure you'll walk again."

"Nora, after I'm gone, I want you to remember how much I loved rooming with you. You made me laugh, filled our room with light."

"After you're gone? So, you're planning on breaking out of here before me, huh? Well, that's good. You just keep thinking positive." Nora smiled at Lila and truly did hope this sweet child she'd come to love would quickly regain her ability to walk.

"It won't be long. Only not the way you think." A tear drizzled down the side of Lila's face.

"What are you talking about?" A warning flared inside Nora.

"There's more wrong with me than stiff muscles. It feels like my whole insides are rocks."

"Oh, Lila, that's probably just constipation." Nora giggled.

Lila laughed and closed her eyes. "See, that's why Stella calls you Sunshine."

Nora didn't feel light at the moment. A black blanket seemed to descend from the ceiling and cover their beds. Neither spoke again before she fell asleep.

* * * * *

The day Lila died, Nora felt a piece of her die as well. She'd never had a chance to hold hands with this sister she'd never had, this dear friend, this partner in crime. She'd never told Lila she loved her, or that she would miss her.

Why does losing someone you love hurt more than losing your own legs?

Dave no longer came around. *Why would he?* For that matter, Nora's brother Mike had quit coming with Mom, Dad, and Donny on Sunday afternoons. Minutes dragged into hours. Hours stretched into interminably long days between Sundays.

Although she could now sit with pillows propped behind her back, she could bend her right arm at the elbow, and hold a cup in her right hand, her legs still proved useless. That's why she was shocked when Stella stormed in announcing Nora was on her way to a heated swimming pool.

Loaded onto a stretcher, Nora was wheeled into a waiting ambulance. Off they went. The fast-moving vehicle made her dizzy. She couldn't recall ever getting dizzy lying down before. Nearing the city pool, *it* occurred to her, and would soon be obvious to others. Embarrassment over her withered, bony legs and arms swallowed her. *They'll stare and laugh.* Dressed in shorts and a tee-shirt—without a brassiere no less—Nora cringed at her image. If only she could run away. *Ha. That's a joke. If I could run, I wouldn't be in this predicament in the first place.*

She closed her eyes and whisked herself away onto her bicycle. Down Smithy's Hill. The wind in her face renewed her spirit. Her legs pumped, sending her faster and faster, until she fairly flew down the steep slope. At the bottom she raced through the intersection without regard for oncoming traffic. She was in charge now, so automobiles would have to stop for her. On she went, onto the gravel country road, heading for the Platte River. It was autumn and cottonwood's shiny, yellow leaves shimmered in the sun against a clear, blue sky. She breathed deeply, filling her lungs with crisp, fall air. On both sides of the road, cornstalk stubbles littered field after field. Fat cattle grazed amongst the rows, confirming this year's bumper crop. Peddling the last mile to the river, she coasted here and there, stopping only to observe a rooster pheasant scurry down a corn row, pecking unharvested grain here and there. Sun glinted off the bright green and blue of his neck feathers. Varying shades of gold layers clothing his body caught the light as well. Something startled him and he took flight, spreading his wings into the slight breeze. For that moment, Nora sailed with him, up, up, and away into freedom.

Landing in warm water, she opened her eyes and startled at the sea of bodies mirroring her own. Not trusting her emotions, she avoided eye contact, lest she discover a familiar face.

"Welcome to swim therapy." A young woman reached for Nora's hand and shook it before directing the men carrying her gurney to float it between two rails. The woman eased into the water and glided in beside Nora. "Hi, I'm Barbara. Now that you have some strength in your arms and hands, you're ready to learn to balance yourself. The water will help keep you up." Barbara gently swung Nora's legs off the stretcher. "Can you lift your hands onto the rails?"

With some difficulty, Nora swung her right hand up and onto the rail. Her left hand resisted. Barbara waited, not offering to help. *I want to do this on my own, anyway.* By the time she had accomplished the task, Nora was exhausted.

The men removed the stretcher completely. For the first time since Polio had taken residence in her body, Nora stood upright. Well, standing wasn't exactly the right word, but at least she was in an almost vertical position. Her head swooned. She felt like she was going to faint.

Barbara grabbed hold of her. "A little light-headed?" That's normal. Your body isn't used to this quite yet."

"I feel like I'm going to throw up." Nora swallowed hard against the rising nausea.

"Don't close your eyes. And don't look down at the water. Focus on me." Barbara embraced her hands around Nora's waist while stepping back.

Nora's arms quivered. Despite the water buoying the majority of her weight, the pressure requiring her arms to support her proved to be unbearable. Sweat erupted from her pores.

Letting go, Barbara ducked under one rail and came up behind Nora. "I'm going to hold you while you try to bob. Ease up on your arms and let your body drop just a little. See if you can push even slightly against the bottom of the pool with your feet."

At first Nora needed Barbara's help. Soon, she found she could bob up and down, using her feet to push off, then working her hands and arms to raise up. Watching others in the pool doing the same, she realized it looked a lot easier than it was. Almost completely spent, she wanted to quit. And yet she didn't. Like Stella had said, "Step by step." Nora hummed *Itsy Bitsy Spider*.

That night, she slept soundly. In fact, for the next several weeks, with days jammed with hard labor, each night brought her more restful sleep. It all proved to be fruitful labor. By the end of her fourth month in the hospital, she was ready to go home. Although not able to walk, at least she could stand.

Stella and the physical therapist had reviewed Nora's workouts with her mom, who promised to faithfully adhere to the regimen.

Now that "D" Day—Dismissal Day—had finally arrived, Nora proudly swung her legs over the side of the bed, braced her arms on the wheelchair, pivoted, and plopped onto the seat. She had even built up enough strength to wheel herself down the hall, and would have except for Donny wanting to steer her all the way out to their auto. She gladly accepted his offer since she had not yet wheeled further than the end of the corridor and back to her room.

Loading the wheelchair into the Plymouth's trunk ended up in a cumbersome wrestling match between the chair and her dad. She was thankful he had brought bailing twine to fasten the lid shut. The ride home was more awkward than Nora had imagined it would be. Mom tried to act like everything was back to normal; Donny got yelled at when he smacked Dad in the back of the head with one of Nora's crutches. Dad still couldn't look at Nora without overwhelming sadness. Nora breathed a sigh of relief when they finally pulled onto the frozen-mud-rutted lane leading to their house. Snow had melted on the road, but along the shoulders dirty mounds of the once-white powder lumped up like camel humps.

Nora's relief was short-lived. Getting to the house from the muddy driveway in her wheelchair posed a problem, as did using crutches. Finally, Dad scooped her up, carried her to the kitchen, and set her down on an aluminum chair like she was made of porcelain.

"Dad, I won't break." Nora chuckled but clipped it short when she saw no one else laughed. "Watch." She gathered her crutches and pulled herself into standing position. Slowly, she made her way around the table by dragging her feet, supporting most of her weight with her arms. She was glad for recent strength in her right leg, as it allowed her to actually stand, with crutches of course.

Mom clapped. "Look, John!"

Nora forced a smile at Mom's attempts to turn Dad's sadness into gladness—or something other than the despair weighing him down.

In the wheelchair, Donny zipped around the table and caught Nora's left crutch. Down Nora went. Mom screamed in horror. Upstairs, Mike's bedroom door slammed. Dad yelled at Donny. Donny jumped up and ran crying from the room.

"It's okay. I'm used to it." Nora tried desperately to restore order but the damage was done. Nothing she could say or do—save walking, jumping, skipping, and such—would bring normalcy to the Parrish household.

Dad picked up Nora and sat her in her wheelchair. "Guess I'd better get out to the barn. Elsie got into some barbed wire. Got to keep salve on her cuts." The door closed quickly behind him.

Mom scurried to the refrigerator. "Are you hungry? We've got to fatten you up."

"No. I'm a little tired. I think I'll just go up to my room." Suddenly, Nora realized what she'd said. A room on the second floor of the old farmhouse.

Mom swooped in to sweep aside the awkward silence. "I moved everything down to our room. Well, now your bedroom. Dad and I switched with you. We re-wallpapered. You're going to love it." She motioned for Nora to follow.

Right behind her, Nora got as far as the doorway between the kitchen and living room. The narrow frame prohibited the wheelchair's passage. "Now what?" Exasperated, Nora burst into tears.

A knock at the door silenced her.

Without waiting to be let in, Jean and Patsy bounced into the kitchen carrying a butcher-paper-Crayon-decorated banner. WELCOME HOME, NORA!

Nora quickly swiped away her tears and spread her arms for hugs. "Boy, oh boy, are you two a sight for sore eyes."

Jean kneeled to embrace Nora. "When are you coming back to school?" Jean asked.

Hesitantly, Patsy edged closer to the two. "You . . . you're in a wheelchair."

Mom stepped in behind Nora. "Of course, this is only temporary."

Embarrassed by the defensive tone of untruth in her mom's voice, Nora started to say something, but Patsy spoke first. "When they said you were coming home from the hospital, I . . . I just assumed you . . . you were healed."

"I am. That is, I'm much better. I can even walk—sort of—with crutches. I don't need this old thing." Nora slapped the wheelchair's arm and rose unsteadily to her feet. "Where are my crutches?" As Jean handed first one then the other to her, Nora couldn't help but notice Jean couldn't—or wouldn't—make eye contact.

Patsy glanced at her watch. "Oh dear. We've got to be going. Cheerleading practice is in ten minutes."

Jean cleared her throat and shifted feet. "No, it's—"

Patsy cut Jean off. "You must not have gotten the message." Patsy tugged Jean's sleeve.

Jean, it seemed to Nora, struggled for words, but ended up saying no more than "Well, see y—" before Patsy dragged her out the door.

Through blurred vision Nora dragged herself on crutches to her new bedroom and propped herself in front of the dresser mirror. She studied her withered body, then her face. *What do you see, Nora? A pathetic cripple?* Closing her eyes, her brother Mike, Dad, Mom, Jean, and Patsy came instantly to mind. Before her flashed faces of denial, pity, embarrassment, discomfort, and repulsion.

Polio, what a crippler. For everyone.

Nora swiveled on her good leg and leaned her crutches against the wall. Flopping across her bed, she closed her eyes to reality and sailed down Smithy's Hill.

"DAISIES FOR MAMA"

"Bucky, 1949's our toughest year yet." Pop pushes a smile. "But by the time you're seven, Mama will be home and good as ever." Pop's hand comes off the steering wheel and plops on my head. He shuffles my hair, which hasn't been combed in a couple days. I'll slick it down once we get there.

Me'n Pop barrel down the dirt road in our Stoody-baker that Mama calls Champ. A picture of Mama fuzzes in my head, then unblurs, kind of like when I snap-shotted her in my Brownie box-camera before she left. My throat swells shut. I stare out the window. Fence posts flick by.

"STOP!" I shout.

Pop clobbers the brake. "What the—?" he asks, not exactly in his friendliest voice. Champ fishtails from ditch to ditch. Dust clouds gulp us up. Mama calls Kansas the grime capital of the world.

"DAISIES!" I yell and point to a whole field of 'em.

Be quick about it," Pop says.

I zip back with a fistful of Mama's favorite flowers. She says posies are good medicine.

Pop shifts Champ into first, second, and third. We're off.

So are my shoes and socks. I kick them off to clean out the weeds and burrs they picked up in the field.

It's a long way to get to Mama. I can't keep my eyes open. When I wake up Mama's flowers are wilted over in my fist. I feel like crying but I have to be a big boy for her.

We climb the steps of the tall, brick building. The cement steps are hot against the soles of my feet.

In the lobby, a nurse eyeballs me and my dirty feet. "Children aren't allowed in. Tuberculosis is highly contagious."

I start to cry; I can't help it.

The nurse looks at my daisies. "I'm a Daisy, too." She points to her nametag. "Daisybelle," she says, like I can't read.

Well, I can't make out the whole word. It has too many letters in it.

"Let's give these a drink." She snatches Mama's flowers out of my hand. "They'll be fresh as new in no time. Daisies are *just* what the doctor ordered," she says.

"He must've ordered lots." I point to a vase of 'em on the counter.

Daisybelle laughs and whispers to Pop.

Pop winks. "Come with me, son." He takes me around back of the sani-terrarium. Underneath a balcony, we wait on the thickest, greenest grass I've ever seen. I squish it between my bare toes.

Pretty soon, Daisy wheels Mama out onto the ledge above us. Mama spots me making grass angels. I hope they're as good as the snow angels I made with her last winter, before she got sick.

Mama holds my daisies up, fresh as ever.

My heart does a somersault.

She smiles, goes into a coughing fit, then blows me a kiss.

It floats down and I catch it and smack it on my cheek. My face feels hot. But it's a good kind of hot. Posies *are* good medicine.

Pop's right. Mama will be home for my seventh birthday.

READER'S GUIDE

OVERALL QUESTIONS FOR DISCUSSION

1. How appropriately titled is the book?

2. Does the author achieve her purpose in writing these stories as she mentions in the Preface?

3. How do the stories tie together?

4. How original and unique is this book?

5. What makes the settings important?

6. What was your initial reaction in reading the stories, and what feelings did the stories evoke in you?

7. In what ways do you relate to the characters?

8. Which characters do you like best and why?

9. Which story in this collection is your favorite and why?

10. What new things did you learn?

11. Do you believe any of the stories could be expanded into a full-length book?

12. What question(s) would you like to ask the author?

13. In crafting each story in this compilation, the author
     includes actual historical events and conveys the
     innocence of children caught in the turmoil, tragedies,
     and triumphs of the 1940s. In addition to story plots,
     the author delivers a unique point of view from each
     protagonist, intentionally including only a minimal
     physical description of each character—with the hope
     that the distinctive voices will evoke an emotional
     experience and vivid images for readers.
     How does this work for you?

14. Had these stories been told from an omniscient or adult
     perspective, what do you believe would have been lost in
     the telling?

Story-Specific Questions

From one story to the next, the narratives render a compare and contrast of circumstances, location, and the child's voice:

1940

"Footsteps in the Night"

"Footsteps in the Night" is told in Nicolette's first person point of view, in past tense, i.e. "I was." However, Nicolette concludes her story a few years later in the present tense of "I am."

1.   How does this writing technique affect your reading of and reaction to the story?

2.   What drew you into the narrative and kept you reading?

"In No time in Nowhere"

Lily moves with her family from Boston to rural Oklahoma so her father can avoid involvement in an impending war. In the previous story, Nicolette goes with her family from Paris to rural southern France, her father moving them out of the dangerous Occupied Zone to a safer location. Yet neither setting is free from threats for the girls. Lily encounters a schoolyard bully in contrast to the previous story of Nicolette coming face to face with German soldiers. Even at an early age children learn coping mechanisms, the most important of which is playing roles or games.

1.   How does each girl use this coping mechanism to adapt to her relocation?

2.   What technique does each employ when she comes face to face with jeopardy?

3.   What changes Lily's opinion and feelings about Elmer?

1941

"Dear Dad"

In contrast to the previous storylines, the author fashions letters from Junior for the telling of this story, his voice being distinctive and personal.

1.   How effective is this writing method in engaging you in an emotional experience, i.e. how do you feel about Junior in just a few pages?

2.   What was your reaction to the mid-sentence ending of the letter?

1942

"Brother's Keeper"

However implausible it may seem, boys not yet of mandatory age did go off to war in this era. Willie believes he is sacrificing his life for his older but weaker brother.

1. Which brother do you think the story's title refers to? Or perhaps both? If so, how and why?

2. How would you compare and contrast Willie and Tommy?

3. What individual personality characteristics help them adapt, both in childhood after the loss of their mother, and after the death of their father?

1943

"Belly of Earth"

It is fact that families did escape Nazi invasion by hiding in fields and caves—for months, as well as beyond a year's time. The weather, famine, and fear they endured is unimaginable. The author employs broken-English to create a realistic telling of "Belly of Earth."

1. How does this way of speaking work for you?

2. What keeps Casimir's hope alive?

3. Grandmother states they are "marinating in belly of earth." To marinate is to soak in order to flavor or soften something. Symbolically, how can you apply this to Casimir?

"Berta's Questions"

Whereas in "Belly of Earth" Casimir is confined in a dark cave, in "Berta's Questions," Berta is free, yet confined to the belly of a concentration camp where darkness prevails.

1. Berta's aunt makes a choice between her soon-to-be husband and her niece. What reasons might *Tante* Frieda have had which influenced her decision to leave Berta at a concentration camp with her father?

2. Berta's dying mother charged Berta with righting wrongs. What might have her mother been thinking to put this burden on a child?

3. From where does Berta muster courage to carry out her mother's bidding?

4. What do you think is Berta's most profound question?

1944

"Internment Camp"

1. Kayori (Kay) does not identify with the other Japanese in the internment camp. Why?

2. What coping mechanisms help her endure this imprisonment, i.e. how is she able to escape her environment if only temporarily?

3. Is Kay being realistic in her fear that her best friend, Shirley may not look at her with the "same eyes" upon her return?

"Playing War"

Children are casualties of war in many different ways. Playing war is one means by which Henri can take part in what he has seen—and perhaps make peace with it, or at best, minimize the chaos in his world.

1. How does Henri's innocence defeat this coping mechanism and rob him of peace?

2. How many lives are affected by Henri's actions and in what way?

1945

"daddys little valentine"

1. Although this is the shortest narrative in the book, how effective is three-year-old Pauline's voice in telling the story?

2. Pauline is the purest form of innocence. At what time does a three-year-old stop believing and stop hoping her daddy will come home to her?

3. How might hope, then truth, affect a child's soul and spirit?

"Going Places"

1. In what ways is Addie's world widened by the truckload of Nazi POWs brought to her farm?

2. What contributes to her abandonment of prejudice?

3. Where are the places Addie goes, as suggested in the story's title?

1946

"German Descent"

1. The story opens with Klaudia limping as a result of being hit by a bicycle. At what point might it dawn on her that this may have been more than an accident?

2. Where in the story does the title's double entendre occur to you?

3. Claudia's innocence is a heartening protector. When does it no longer shield her from harsh reality?

"Smokin' 'Em"

In contrast to "German Descent," Digger's world is fairly normal and without deprivation or trouble—except of his own making.

1. How does the residue of WWII figure into his life in rural North Dakota?

2. Digger fantasizes going off to war and becoming a hero. How does this promote his sense of self-esteem and control over his life?

3. Digger relies on the defense mechanism of lying to dig his way out of messes. How does this work out for him?

1947

"Upstart or New Start?"

1. Initially, Maxine (Max) has no say in the change in her environment. What does she do to establish her voice and adapt so quickly to her new life?

2. How does this reflect and/or encompass the story's title?

3. How does her dedication to her job as counter clerk help restore family unity?

"Brooklyn vs. the Bronx"

The previous story, "Upstart or New Start?" takes place on the west coast of the United States. "Brooklyn vs. the Bronx" transpires on the east coast. Both Max and Francis develop unique voices which embrace local lingo of the time. Perhaps this is a coping mechanism that helps them feel more adult and in control of themselves and their circumstances.

1.   What effect does this have on the telling of their stories?

2.   When his father is killed in the war, even at ten, Francis desperately needs to be head of the household. The intrusion of his mother's fiancé threatens Francis' status in the home. How is he able to let go of this position without compromising his self-esteem?

"Chief Lesson"

1.   What lessons do Ruby and Polly learn from their mothers?

2.   What wisdom does Ruby demonstrate at twelve years of age?

1948

"Orphanage"

In preparation for this story, the author spoke with individuals who had been put in orphanages during this decade. Although the story and characters are fictional, some of the conditions in "Orphanage" reflect these personal accounts. The measuring of the window shade is one such truth.

1.   It is difficult for Rose to take care of her younger sisters when she has no say over their environment. Initially, Rose accepts this charge her mother gives her, but then is burdened by it. However, she perseveres. What helps her continue to care and do the best she can?

2.   With what life lessons does Rose leave the orphanage?

1949

"Crippler"

When a child is disabled, her world and sense of self change. How she meets this challenge is an individual choice. Nora refuses to adopt a victim mentality.

1.   What coping mechanisms does Nora embrace and employ to meet her limitations head on and help her rise, (pardon the play on words), above them?

2.   Does Nora's sense of humor keep her in denial or work to her benefit?

3.   How does this affect others' treatment of her?

"Daisies for Mama"

Bucky's innocence and belief in the healing power of his flowers shape his world.

1.   How uplifting must this be to his sick mother, especially when she sees the grass angels Bucky makes for her?

2.   In the earlier story, "Dear Dad," Junior mentions a Studebaker Champion automobile he saw advertised in a magazine. Did you make the connection to Bucky's Mom's nickname, "Champ," for their car—the Stoody-baker as Bucky calls it?

3.	What effect does Bucky's flowers and angels have on you?

4.	Both Nora in "Crippler" and Bucky in this story live on hope. Is hope all they have? If not, what other things in their lives do they cling to which help them move forward?

ABOUT THE AUTHOR

Mary Stone is an inspiring keynote speaker and author.

She began her career in higher education after earning a Master's Degree in Counseling at the University of Nebraska, Kearney.

Lower Columbia College in Longview, Washington conferred upon her Faculty Emeritus for her years of outstanding and dedicated service in teaching and counseling. In addition to her career as a college Counselor, Mary practiced as a Licensed Mental Health Therapist for many years.

Mary loves to write, garden, travel, do puzzles, and spend time with her family—not necessarily in that order, depending on the day and on the Pacific Northwest weather.

She and her husband make their home in Washington state.

Mary invites you to contact her
at: maryellenstone@hotmail.com or at
her website: https://marystonewriter.com